Kenilworth

and

The Great War

KENILWORTH AND THE GREAT WAR

A Tribute to the Fallen

Susan Tall

Betty Sunley

CLOCK TOWER PUBLICATIONS

First published in 2004 by
Clock Tower Publications
21 Laburnum Avenue
Kenilworth
Warwickshire
CV8 2DR
UK

ISBN: 0-9548689-0-0

*Front Cover: Taken from a postcard of Warwick Road
in the early part of the 20th Century*

Back Cover: The War Memorial, 2004, photo Betty Sunley

Prepared by David Tall using an Apple Macintosh Computer in Adobe *InDesign*®, using 12 pt Palatino font; pictures processed in Adobe *Photoshop*®.

Printed by Warwick Printing Company Ltd, Caswell Road, Leamington Spa, Warwickshire, CV31 1QD, UK.

The 120 millimetre, bronze Memorial Plaque, here reproduced at its actual size, was awarded to the next-of-kin of those who lost their lives on active service in the First World War. The one above is in memory of Bertie Bannard from Albion Street, Kenilworth, who died in action on 13th August, 1917.

Contents

Preface

The Kenilworth War Memorial stands proudly at the top of Abbey End, overlooking the Abbey Fields, bearing the names of local people who gave their lives in the two World Wars. As the millenium approached, we began to research those who died during the Great War, beginning what became a long journey of discovery that lasted over five years. It was so compelling that we decided to focus not just on those listed, but on the effects of the war on our town.

In 1914, Kenilworth was a small country town of about six thousand people, still based on a rural economy, with market gardens, fellmongers removing wool from sheepskins, tanneries, brickyards using local clay and a range of other trades. When war was declared, young men flocked to fight for King and country in a spirit of optimism that slowly darkened into a realisation of the slaughter of war. As young soldiers died, Military Tribunals were set up, first to encourage, then to instruct, men to enlist. Those left at home had to take on new responsibilities, with women and children contributing by caring for the wounded, gathering harvests, and coping with food shortages. The tannery prepared leather for the war effort and factories in nearby Birmingham and Coventry manufactured weapons.

After hostilities ended, the joy of victory was soon tempered by the realities of the economic climate. Unemployment and lack of funds limited the people's desire to commemorate those who had fallen. As we read the newspaper accounts of the time, we were surprised to find the War Memorial was the least desired of several schemes. Returning soldiers wished to build a hall for their activities, but found appeals stifled by limited finances. The actions of one man caused everything to fall into place. Charles Randall, Managing Director of the Tannery and Chairman of Kenilworth Council provided personal finance to secure the purchase of new premises for the Working Men's Club, a hall and offices for the British Legion, and chaired the committee that organised the building of the War Memorial.

Our sources of information were wide and varied. As well as the Memorial itself, our major inspiration was the St Nicholas' Church Roll of Honour. This includes information about all those on the town War Memorial, together with names and details of others linked to Kenilworth who died as a result of the war. Local libraries contain newspaper archives, including The Kenilworth Advertiser and the Coventry Herald. We were also kindly lent documents, photographs and letters by relatives and local residents.

Details of most soldiers can be found online, especially on the Commonwealth War Graves Commission site at www.cwgc.org. However, these records rely partly on information from families and are not always accurate or complete. Indeed, all sources needed to be treated carefully as they often contained small differences. Other information came from the 1891 and 1901 censuses; local trade directories; letters, photographs and memorabilia kept by soldiers' families; and soldiers' letters published in local newspapers. These sources have enabled us to build a picture of activities in Kenilworth during the war, enriched with personal stories. However, even after five years of research, there are still individuals for whom we have very brief details, and some who have yet to be positively identified.

The first appendix lists everyone on the war memorial with military and personal details, and a photograph where available. The second lists other individuals linked with Kenilworth who died as a result of the war. The third is a chronological list of the fallen revealing the cumulative losses as the war progressed. The fourth lists primary and secondary sources.

If any reader has additional photographs or information about anyone mentioned we would be very pleased to receive these. We will be maintaining a web-site with up-to-date information and further details as they become available at:

www.kenilworth-war-memorial.org.uk

We hope that our project will act as a testament to those from Kenilworth who so bravely gave their lives during the course of a terrible war, the likes of which the world had never previously experienced. Their moving stories touched us deeply. We will always remember them and trust that future generations will do likewise.

Susan Tall	Betty Sunley
21 Laburnum Avenue	11a Barrow Rd
Kenilworth	Kenilworth
CV8 2DR	CV81EH

Acknowledgements

First and foremost we thank Jenny Morris who had the original idea to research the names on Kenilworth War Memorial. What Jenny saw as just a few months' work turned out to be five years of time-consuming, yet very pleasurable, research and writing. We hope that she will be pleased with the result and thank her for her support.

Numerous people have answered our various pleas for information and photographs and we would particularly like to thank the following, with apologies to any we might have inadvertently missed out:

Mr Neil Collett, the late Mr Dan Bench, Mr John Drew, Mrs Peggy Finch, Mrs Peggy Gamble, Mrs Jacqui Hancox, Mr Phil Haycock, Mr John & Mrs Jean Heatley, Mr W. Hewitt, Mrs Vera Jaye, Mrs Anne Jones, Mrs Vera Martin and the late Mr Charles Martin, the late Miss Joyce Powell, Mr Alan Reed, Mrs Helen Scott, Mrs Chris Selwood, Miss Sally Taylor, Mr J. E. Whateley, plus several members of the Kenilworth branch of the Birmingham & Midland Society for Genealogy & Heraldry.

For allowing us to take photographs of local memorials we would like to thank: Kenilworth Post Office, Kenilworth Working Men's Club, Kenilworth St. Nicholas' Church, Kenilworth St. John's Church, Kenilworth Methodist Church.

We also thank:

The British Library Newspaper Library, Colindale, for allowing us to use extracts and photographs from The Kenilworth Advertiser, Coventry Herald, Coventry Graphic and Warwick Advertiser.

Kenilworth Reference Library
Coventry Reference Library
Warwick Reference Library
Royal Warwickshire Regimental Museum
The Commonwealth War Graves Commission
Warwickshire County Record Office for the following photographs:
on page 30, ref. C362 BVI, p.75   on page 33, ref. PH352/71/16
on page 57, ref. C362 BVI, p.77   on page 79, ref. PH352/101/117
on page 91, ref. PH352/101/113

Last but not least, very many thanks are due to Professor David Tall for typesetting the book and preparing the illustrations for publication. Without his invaluable assistance and encouragement this book might not have seen the light of day.

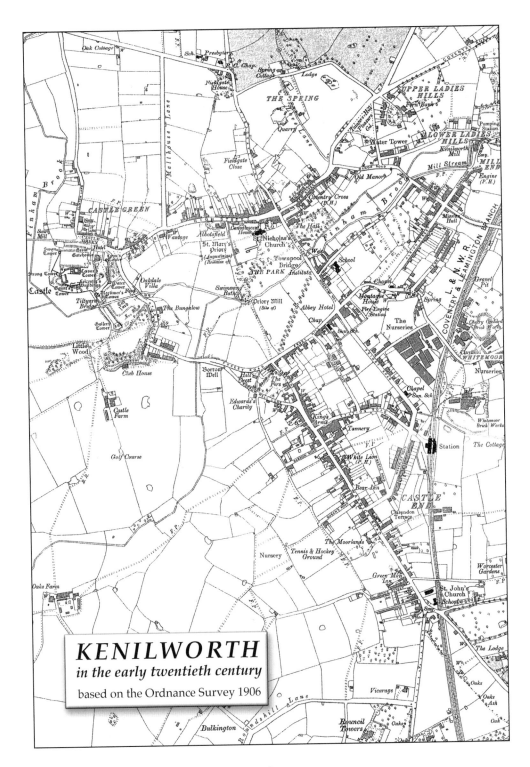

KENILWORTH
in the early twentieth century
based on the Ordnance Survey 1906

Chapter 1

The Town and its People

The small town of Kenilworth in leafy Warwickshire has always had a romantic image, based on its ruined castle with connections to Queen Elizabeth I and Robert Dudley, Earl of Leicester, immortalised in the novel of Sir Walter Scott.

At the beginning of the twentieth century, the Castle was open daily, except for Sundays and Christmas day, at an entrance fee of 6 pence. The modern counter attraction of Warwick Castle was then still a private residence, so Kenilworth Castle, with its dramatic ruins, its grassy slopes inviting picnics, and the peculiar sound bowl of 'Echo Meadow', made it an attractive destination for day-trippers.

At holiday times, hundreds of visitors would flock to the town, many travelling by train from Coventry or Birmingham, whilst others cycled or walked. They came not only to visit the castle but also to see the picturesque ruins of the abbey destroyed by Henry VIII and, in hot weather, many took the opportunity to bathe in the outdoor swimming pool in Abbey Fields.

Kenilworth Castle from the South East

The Town

To this day Kenilworth retains its rural setting in the Warwickshire countryside, its central feature being the Castle and the Abbey Fields, with the Finham Brook running through it, splitting the town into two parts, the old Kenilworth around Castle Green, High Street and St Nicholas' Church, the other running along Warwick Road to the west, spreading to Waverley Road, Priory Road, and around the cluster of streets to the east of Abbey Fields.

At the beginning of the twentieth century the town was much smaller than it is now, with a population of 4,544 in the census of 1901 and 5,774 in April 1911. The three major housing estates that surround Kenilworth today, around Malthouse Lane to the north, Windy Arbour to the east, and the Oaks Estate to the west were yet to be built.

To the west of Warwick Road, both Barrow Road and Queen's Road led to the open countryside. At the southern end of Warwick Road, opposite St John's Church, in St John's Street, Cross Row and White's Row there were houses for the families of working men. The people living here were known as 'Jackenders' (Jack being the diminutive pet-name for someone called John). Others lived in cottages scattered around the town, and in the cluster of roads around School Lane, Park Road, Albion Street extending down Stoneleigh Road to Mill End, Spring Lane, Henry Street, Arthur Street, and Whitemoor Road.

High Street at the turn of the century

The People

Before the Great War, the green oasis of Abbey Fields was encircled by grand houses accommodating wealthier inhabitants, along High Street in the old town, down Bridge Street and round the top of Abbey Hill, along Borrowell Lane, Castle Road and back to Castle Green. Other large houses were to be found in the outer reaches of the town, in places such as Coventry Road or Glasshouse Lane.

Kenilworth was a desirable place to live for the landed gentry and for the richer industrialists who ran factories in nearby Coventry and Birmingham. Lord Ernest Seymour, JP, a former Lord Lieutenant of the county and a member of the aristocratic Seymour family of Ragley Hall near Alcester, lived with his wife, Lady Georgiana, and family at The Firs, in Abbey End, on a large plot of land now occupied by the De Montfort Hotel. Lord and Lady Seymour were very public-spirited; he was Chairman of the local Conservative and Unionist Club whilst she was Vice-President of the Warwickshire Branch of the Red Cross Society, President of the Kenilworth Maternity Association and had links with the Girls' Reformatory School and the Kenilworth Convalescent Home.

Several industrialists lived in the same area. William T. Pears, JP, of Pear's Soap fame resided at The Hall in Bridge Street, now turned into flats and overlooking the appropriately named Pears Close.

Warwick Road

George M. Turner lived at Montpelier House in Abbey Hill. He was a generous benefactor to the town, having donated the clock tower in The Square, as well as the new screen at St Nicholas' church.

Along Coventry Road was Crackley Hall (now the site of St Joseph's School), occupied by George Winstanley, a wealthy gas engineer.

The Gables, Crackley, was the home of Frank Dudley Docker, chairman of the Birmingham-based Metropolitan Amalgamated Railway Carriage and Wagon Company (now Metro-Cammell), which built most of the British tanks for the Great War.

Charles Randall, the manager director of Kenilworth Tannery, the town's largest employer, lived at The Limes in Warwick Road. As the war progressed, he was to become Chairman of the Council and the benefactor to a wide range of causes in the town, including the Town War Memorial.

Lincoln Chandler, who moved to the town in 1903 to work for Mr Docker, lived at Abbotsfield in High Street. He had started his working life as an engineer's clerk and had now risen to the post of managing director of Mr Docker's company at its Saltley Works. He took his civic duties seriously, becoming a town councillor in 1910, the Vice Chairman of the Kenilworth Working Men's Club, and later the commander of the Kenilworth Volunteer Corps during the war.

The local doctor, Dr Reginald Tweedy, lived at Abbey House in Abbey Hill. Next door, in a house named Belmont, lived an architect, Harry Quick, who was responsible for many designs in Kenilworth, including the screen inside St Nicholas' church and the Parochial Hall.

On the outskirts of the town at Woodside, Glasshouse Lane, lived Albert Cay, JP, a Birmingham glass manufacturer, with his wife Annie, the daughter of Sir John Jaffray (one of the proprietors of the *Birmingham Daily Post* and a former High Sheriff of Warwickshire). Mr and Mrs Cay were great benefactors to the town, supporting a range of activities with generous donations. At the beginning of the war they would give over half the fund raised by the town, and after the war, Mrs Cay continued her philanthropy upon the death of her husband, providing the town with its first motorised fire engine and the maternity unit called Cay Block at the Warneford Hospital in Leamington.

Trades and Professions

At the accession of King George V, Kenilworth was a typical farming community with some light industry. Many of the farms, and the castle itself, were owned by the Clarendon estate. Several market gardens cultivated special crops of strawberries, tomatoes, cucumbers and flowers under glass and sent their produce to London by train. On the land now named Whateley's Drive were the glasshouses where Mr Whateley grew his famous orchids. In 1910, three tons of chrysanthemums were dispatched to London on a busy railway line that was an important link for the town long before the demise of the railways under Lord Beeching's axe in the 1960s.

The principal industries were the tanning of leather at the Tannery, situated on the present-day site of Talisman Square and, at Mill End, the production of cattle-feed cake and fellmongering, which prepared animal skins for leather-making. These provided ready employment for the workers living around the town, but as time passed, the higher wages available in the growing car industry in Coventry began to tempt men away to work in the nearby city.

There was also a wide spectrum of trades in the town. In Albion Street alone, Spennell's directory of 1910 included a clockmaker, wheelwright, gardener, music teacher, signalman, labourer, waggoner,

Albion Street

bricklayer, laundress, motor engineer, butcher, dressmaker, painter, grocer and carpenter. At the end of the street, in a building now used by the British Legion, stood the Police Station, manned by Inspector Parkinson and his two constables.

In 1911 a town crier was appointed. He had no salary but was provided with a uniform and used the Clerk of the Council's bell.

Kenilworth at this time had its own council – the Kenilworth Urban District Council, consisting of 12 Councillors with Dr William Growse JP, as Chairman. Its offices were then in Rosemary Hill, adjacent to the Fire Station. The councillors represented a good cross section of the town's businessmen and tradesmen – the chairman was a surgeon and the others included farmers, a fellmonger, a cabinet-maker, a saddler and a draper.

As in any small rural community, individuals grouped together in activities for the common good. These included institutions such as the Working Men's Club, the Conservative Club, the Oddfellows, Druids and other friendly societies.

For leisure there were always the local public houses, contributing not only to an occasional exuberance that might lead to drunkenness or rowdy behaviour, but also to genuine acts for the good of the community. A collection for the Saturday Hospital Collection, in August 1912, for example, raised £49. 14s. 5d, from public houses, businesses and private individuals, including contributions from:

Clarendon Inn	The Tannery, Warwick Rd
Wyandotte Inn	Mr G. Eagles, Oil Cake Manufacturer, Mill End
Coventry Cross Inn	Mr H. Lawrence, Builder, Warwick Rd
Malt Shovel Inn	Messrs Street & Wamsley, Mill End
Albion Tavern	The Old Brickyard
Queen & Castle Hotel	Castle Gate Box, per Mr Hirons
Engine Inn	Cherry Orchard Brickyard, Whitemoor
White Lion Inn	The Kennels
Bear Inn	The Currusal Tanyard
Cottage Inn	Urban District employees
Virgin's Inn	Miss Stroudley, Park Rd, P.O. & Stores, Park Rd
King's Arms Hotel	Mr T. Dickenson, Plumber, The Square
Earl Clarendon	Miss Jebbett, Priory Row
The Globe	Miss Satchwell's Tea Rooms, Castle Green
The Green Man	Co-operative Stores, Park Rd.

The Law

Kenilworth had its own Divisional Sessions and Children's Court to deal with minor offences. Drunkenness was usually punished by a fine. A man drunk and disorderly outside the King's Arms Hotel was fined 10 shillings, another leaving the Bear Inn was fined 20 shillings. One Leamington man, convicted over eighty times, was found drunk on waste land and conveyed to the Police Station on a handcart.

Inspector Parkinson, giving evidence against Sidney Aitkin of White's Row and Arthur Farren of Albion Street, declared indecent language to be a prevalent offence in Kenilworth. Both were fined 10 shillings. Another offender was fined 5 shillings with 7 shillings costs.

Begging was considered a more serious offence, usually punished by a prison sentence of a week to a month, often with hard labour. Sergeant Butcher reported that local shops were 'worried to death by beggars' and it was not unusual for both men and women to be imprisoned on conviction.

Even though motorised transport was only a fraction of what it is today, traffic offences were a regular occurrence. A man was fined 10 shillings for being in charge of a horse and trap in Warwick Road without having proper control. An engineer who drove a motorcycle 'in a dangerous manner' was fined £2.2s, with the Bench commenting that '20 miles an hour was an excessive speed.' Charles Fulford was fined 14 shillings with 7 shillings costs for riding a bicycle without a light, even though he pleaded not guilty and presented evidence in the form of a bottle with a candle in its neck.

There were also the usual civil misdemeanours and petty thefts. A man summoned for non-payment of matrimonial arrears of £1.8s was jailed for a month. The licensee of the Royal Oak was fined £2.2s for watering down whisky by adding 6% water. An employee of Harry Hincks, the butcher in the Square, was fined 5 shillings for stealing 14 lbs of bones and selling them on for 2d.

In the children's court, those convicted often received corporal punishment. Two lads of about seven years old were charged with stealing coal from John Burman, coal merchant of Abbey End. A neighbour had given them 6d to buy him some coal but they spent the money and attempted to steal the coal instead. One boy received three strokes of the birch, the other six.

More seriously, Violet Emily Williams, a laundress at the Girls' Reformatory School, pleaded guilty to stealing a sovereign from the assistant matron and was sent to the County Quarter Sessions where she received a three-year sentence at a girl's Borstal Institution.

The level of crime was a source of public concern. *The Kenilworth Advertiser* in October 1913 reported, 'The recent burglaries serve to call attention to the fact that there are not enough police in Kenilworth. Although the population had increased by 1,200 since the last census, yet the strength of the police force remains the same. Perhaps the County Council will be approached with a view to an addition.'

Kenilworth in the second decade of the twentieth century was much like any other small rural town in England. It had its less fortunate citizens who fell foul of the law, but it also had great assets in its farming, its light industry and small businesses, with a host of other activities based in its clubs and churches.

Recreation

Recreation was available through clubs for golf, football, cricket, cycling, swimming, bowling, croquet and lawn tennis. Some of these, such as golf, were the preserve of the more wealthy, but many others (such as football or cycling) were available to the wider population.

Public spirited citizens banded together for all kinds of activities, typical events being a Co-operative Society Concert at the Abbey

St Nicholas' Church from the Abbey Fields

Hotel Assembly Room, a presentation of 'The Charge of the Light Brigade' by the Royal Electric Theatre Company at the King's Arms, a Fête at the Castle organized by the Primrose League, a Flower and Poultry Show of the Horticultural Society, a Fête in the Bear Field with such attractions as a cinematograph exhibition and Clark's electrically lighted merry-go-round which delighted adults as well as children.

On special days, trips were organised to take the workers for a brief holiday. Regularly each August, the Tannery took its employees and families on a chartered train for its annual trip to Blackpool. Captain Jackson of the Fire Station and his twenty or so volunteer firemen had regular outings, visiting the White City and Olympia in London. An annual Mop Fair was held in the town each September in the Bear Field off Warwick Road.

The Churches

Many activities in the town revolved around the churches of St Nicholas', St John's, St Barnabas Mission, St Augustine's Catholic Church and the Congregational, Wesleyan, Albion Baptist, and Brethren Chapels. The Christadelphians started holding meetings in the town in 1913.

On the Friday following the death of King Edward VII, all places of business were closed and all places of worship held memorial services.

The regular activities of the churches included fund-raising for repairs and new buildings. In 1910, repairs were completed to St John's Church steeple, which had reportedly de-teriorated to a dangerous state.

St John's Church

At the other end of Kenilworth, St Nicholas' Church sought to raise £80 for the repair of their steeple, and £1800 for a new Parochial Hall. By the next year the cost of the Hall had increased to £2200; but donations of £100 each from Mr George Turner and Mr Dudley Docker, £200 from an anonymous lady, and other activities by the church members raised the total to £2000, so that the work could begin with only £200 outstanding. The new Parochial Hall was opened in October 1911.

The Coronation of King George V

On the 22nd June 1911, Kenilworth celebrated the Coronation of King George V. The townspeople decorated their houses with flags and bunting in national colours. The Square looked very gay with streamers hung across from house to house. Everywhere there was a desire to participate in the general decorative scheme. Services were held in the local churches.

At about 1 o'clock it rained heavily as 500 of the oldest inhabitants were having dinner inside a tent and the water came in.

A procession formed in Southbank Road and was described as one of the best ever held. The Town Band led the parade, followed by many tableaux. The Red Cross took part with attendant nurses and doctors. Sports were held in the Abbey Fields in the afternoon and a bonfire lit in the evening. All school children were given tea and a commemorative mug provided by Councillor Randall.

Mrs Cay of Woodside gave £100 to the Warneford Hospital to mark the event, which was used for a trolley to wheel patients 'into the out-of-doors.' Miss Wilson of Fern Lea, Abbey Hill, gave a Coronation Party for the parishioners of St Nicholas, with music by the Town Band.

Kenilworth responded to its position in the British Empire much as any other town would have done. It enjoyed its holidays and royal celebrations, but it had little awareness of the world outside. *The Kenilworth Advertiser* reported that concern was being expressed in many parts of the country regarding the decline in numbers in the Territorial Force. (The Territorial Army was a volunteer force locally organized to provide a reserve of trained and disciplined manpower for use in an emergency.) Locally, Major Pearson pointed out the difficulties experienced in getting an adequate supply of horses for the Warwickshire Territorials and suggested boldly that they should face the alternative of mechanical traction.

The Kenilworth ford

Day by day the life of the town went on. In July 1912, a storm left a great quantity of water lying in the lower parts of the town. The following month it was reported that 'in the last fortnight we have had snow, hail, thunder, rain and frost. Kenilworth, like the rest of the country, suffers from a surplus of rain.' More rain fell in September with floods in the town and the sad death of a child drowned in the brook in Oxpen Meadow. It was noted that it was the first flood since 1900. Later in the year, the Automobile Association decided to erect a post at the ford by the castle to indicate the depth of water when the brook overflowed.

Kenilworth had a ready supply of water coming not only from the River Avon to the south, but also from boreholes that tapped the water table deep below the town. In 1911, fifty further houses had been connected to the water supply, making 1,183 houses in all. However, in November and December 1913, there were several cases of typhoid fever. The cases were not confined to any particular part of the town.

The local council called two special meetings within a week at which the County Medical Officer and the directors of Kenilworth Water Company were present. A circular was issued advising people to boil their water. The Council declared that they had found the source of the problem; it had been cut off and, by Christmas Day, the whole of the water mains had been disinfected.

On Boxing Day, *The Kenilworth Advertiser* published a letter from Lincoln Chandler declaring that 'the damage being done to Kenilworth is incalculable, and nothing but a strictly independent and official inquiry into the whole question will be satisfactory.' More cases followed in the New Year to make a total of 43, of which 3 were fatal.

At the end of January 1914 it was reported that the water supply was safe. By April the bore hole that was the source of the problem was filled in and new bore holes were completed. The Town Council considered a takeover of the Water Company, which Dudley Docker said would be 'a leap from the frying pan into the fire' in a letter to *The Kenilworth Advertiser* in May. Councillor Dr Growse, now the Vice-Chairman of the Town Council, refuted charges of incompetence and the matter died down. (The Water Company was later purchased by the Council in 1922 for the sum of £20,800.)

A Glorious Summer and the Declaration of War

As summer 1914 approached, the round of activities in Kenilworth resumed its regular rhythm. In May, the Girls' Reformatory School celebrated Empire Day and 'The Glory of the Empire' was extolled by the schools of St Nicholas and St Austin. In June there was an exceptional spell of hot weather and the Swimming Baths enjoyed its highest attendance since it opened in 1896.

Unbeknown to the people of Kenilworth, enjoying themselves in the summer warmth of 1914, events were happening on the other side of Europe which would affect them forever. In far-off Sarajevo on June 18th, Archduke Franz Ferdinand, heir to the Austro-Hungarian throne, and his wife were assassinated by a Serbian student. This was the trigger for war. Austria demanded a part in the investigation into the shooting but when Serbia refused, Austria, backed by Germany, declared war.

On Bank Holiday Monday, August 3rd, the weather was good and the number of visitors to Kenilworth was very large indeed. As *The Advertiser* reported, 'a very orderly crowd they were.' A young Kenilworth couple took advantage of the holiday to be married. Henry Barnett (known as Harry), a 28-year old labourer and 27-year old Amy Stone, both of Whitemoor, were married at St John's Church.

Over the Channel, Germany declared war on France and invaded Belgium on its way to conquer Paris. This invasion flouted the treaty of 1839 which respected Belgian neutrality and the following day, Tuesday, August 4th, Great Britain declared war on Germany.

Chapter 2

1914 – Optimism

To the people of Kenilworth, as everywhere else, the enormity of what was to come did not fully register. Britain was a world power and had faced such difficulties before and had always prevailed. It was thought the war would be very short-lived, probably over in a matter of weeks or months.

Regular soldiers were immediately mobilised and orders for recall sent out to reservists. The number of men in the armed forces had fallen in recent years, particularly since the Boer War. Britain, with no conscription, had a regular army of only 125,000 men at home and 60,000 on garrison duties overseas. Germany, on the other hand, had already mobilised one and a half million men and was rapidly training and equipping more. This shortfall in Britain's numbers caused the new Secretary of State for War, Lord Kitchener, to propose, as a first step, to raise an additional army of 100,000 volunteers.

The response to the call for volunteers by the Kenilworth townspeople was immediate and patriotic, causing *The Kenilworth Advertiser* to proudly report on the 12th September, 'The extraordinary flocking of young men to the Colours. Wonderful enthusiasm pervaded the town during last week, and probably two out of every three single men of suitable age and physical standard joined the forces.'

The local Warwickshire Regiment was already up to its full complement of soldiers, so a large number joined the King's Royal Rifles, whilst others joined the Oxford Light Infantry and the 10th Hussars. The names of 200 Kenilworth men who had enlisted, or were already serving in the Army or Navy, were published in the newspaper, which out of a population of 6000 showed the town's enthusiastic response. A similar situation had happened in the Boer War, when Kenilworth contributed numbers out of all proportion to its population and many who had seen service in South Africa were now willing and keen to re-enlist.

Men of all classes joined immediately. Two of Lord Seymour's sons were already lieutenants with the Royal Navy: Francis, his eldest, on special service on the east coast, Arthur, his youngest, serving on board HMS Espiegle. Dr Tweedy's 19-year old son Trevor was a second-lieutenant in the 6th Territorial Battalion Northumberland Fusiliers and was mobilised on the day war was declared, as was Lincoln Chandler's 23-year old son, Alfred, a captain in the Territorial Force.

Albert Cay's only son, also named Albert, had been a second-lieutenant in the Warwickshire Yeomanry several years previously but had left the country to settle in Canada with his wife Catherine. In May 1914, Catherine was one of 1,012 lives lost on the 'Empress of Ireland' when it sank in the St Lawrence seaway, just off Montreal. It was the world's second biggest shipping disaster after the Titanic. Albert returned to England and, at the outbreak of war, joined the Worcester Yeomanry to serve as an officer alongside his brother-in-law, Captain Leslie Cheape and his cousin, Sir John Henry Jaffray.

Harold Bates, only son of Mr J. H. Bates of White Thorn, Kenilworth, the director of Fletcher Hardware Company in Birmingham, left his career as a civil engineer with the Midland Railway Company at Derby to offer his services. Two weeks later he was given a Second-Lieutenancy in the Royal Engineers.

Harry Barnett, married just the day before the war was declared, was called as a reservist to serve with the Welsh Fusiliers.

His parents, Mr and Mrs Edward Barnett of Whitemoor, had the distinction of having five sons in the army. Arthur was a regular soldier with the Royal Field Artillery stationed in India, James was a member of the Territorial Force, Edward joined the 3rd Battalion Royal Warwickshire Regiment and Walter joined the Durham Light Infantry.

Mrs Sheepy of High Street had four sons and a son-in-law who joined up early in the war. Likewise the four single sons of Mr and Mrs Colman of Waverley Road acted immediately upon Lord Kitchener's call for volunteers. Brothers, brothers-in-law, cousins, neighbours, workmates, all responded.

Five members of the Kenilworth Fire Brigade enlisted, causing Captain Jackson to call upon old firemen to turn out, should the town fire alarm sound.

The British Expeditionary Force in France

Whilst Lord Kitchener's volunteers remained in England for training, the regular and reservist soldiers were sent over to France in early August with the British Expeditionary Force (BEF) under the command of Field Marshall Sir John French. **James Harris,** a Kenilworth postman and a reservist, was amongst them, arriving at Le Havre with his regiment, the 2nd Battalion South Staffordshires, onboard an adapted cattle boat. Little did he know the adventures and tragedies that would befall him in the coming years.

PRIVATE J. HARRIS
(2nd South Staffordshires.)

Within days of arriving in France several local men were participating in the fighting and at least two had been wounded. **William Drane-Overs** of Albion Street sustained a head injury and was sent back to Kenilworth to recover. He was a regular soldier with the 1st Royal Warwickshire Regiment, having enlisted ten years previously, at the age of 17, as a drummer. William went to France with the BEF as a bandsman but would have been utilised as a stretcher-bearer, this task falling to bandsmen when a battalion was in action. Whilst at home he told *The Kenilworth Advertiser* the story of the 1st Warwicks involvement after embarking for France up to the commencement of the fighting at Mons.

> *The 1st Warwicks, left Southampton on Saturday, the 22nd August, on the Caledonia, 1,100 strong, landing at Boulogne at 9 a.m. next morning. We left at 6 p.m. for the frontier, and arrived at camp, close to St Python, at mid-day on Monday. After a march of six miles to our allotted position we rested awhile. In the middle of the night (Monday) we started to march to Mons, where we arrived at 6 a.m. on Tuesday. We were about to have breakfast, when a convoy of French wounded soldiers came along, and we were then ordered to take up a new position, three miles back, where we entrenched near a large farm house. A German aeroplane came over us about two o'clock, and we tried the effect of rifle fire upon it, but with no result, and our position being discovered, shells soon started to drop amongst us from the oncoming Germans, but with no serious results.*

The German infantry advance guards now put in an appearance at 500 to 600 yard distance, and also German patrols, but except for long range rifle fire, the fighting was restricted to the artillery. The enemy concentrated their fire on our lines of entrenchment, and our artillerymen devoted their attention to the oncoming infantry and patrols. I saw several German shells fall right amongst the 3rd Hussars as they passed across open ground but with absolutely no effect. They exploded probably after sinking in the soil.

At 9 o'clock that evening we again received orders to retire, and the movement was completed by 11 o'clock, by which time the German attack was being pressed closer. My company immediately had orders to re-occupy our previous position near the farm house as German Cavalry patrols were around, and we had not been there long before we gave them a taste of rapid fire from the 250 rifles of our company. Their horses stampeded, and we saw several riderless ones.

After all the pickets had retired, my company followed suit, and we marched all through the night, arriving in the vicinity of Cambrai at six o'clock on Wednesday morning, thoroughly tired out with constant marching and fighting, and loss of sleep.

We had just lain down to rest, when I noticed the King's Own Liverpool Regiment digging trenches on the top of a slope which they occupied in front of us, and in a few minutes they were being hard pressed, for the enemy had surprised them and were dropping shrapnel shells and firing with machine guns before the trenches could be dug.

Captain Burnand gave an order to advance to the assistance of the Liverpools, which we did, across cut corn and a swamp. Our Captain Squires, of our platoon, fell with wounds in back and legs. Arriving on top of the hill we kept up heavy rifle fire on the enemy's infantry, who were utilising hedgerows and ditches for cover. The enemy's rifle fire did little damage, but the artillery had our range to a yard, and made the exposed position too hot to hold.

The British losses on this hill were pretty heavy, but our own guns were doing good execution amongst the Germans. We retired in excellent order, and here it was that I got put out of the picture. I was picked up and conveyed with other wounded in motor lorries to a small base hospital four miles back where the serious cases received attention.

In the subsequent Battle of Mons, the British troops inflicted heavy losses on the Germans. Although the German army was much better equipped in artillery the British were far superior in their use of rifles, so much so that at one point the British infantry's shooting was so fast and accurate the Germans believed they were facing massed machine guns. The German artillery, however, was effective and after a series of tactical retirements a general British retreat began, known as the great Retreat from Mons.

Alongside William Drane-Overs with the 1st Royal Warwicks was Private **Austin Martin,** from Spring Lane. He was an 'old soldier', having previously served five years with the regiment and had been on reserve for seven years when war broke out. He was called to the colours and went through the Mons retreat uninjured, but was badly wounded at the Aisne advance with the biceps of his right arm shot away and a bayonet wound to the leg. He had a long and painful hospital experience with his

Austin Martin

arm, undergoing several operations in an attempt to save the limb from amputation. It was saved, but it proved absolutely useless and he was discharged from the Army in March 1916. Back in Kenilworth he managed to find employment as a swimming bath attendant during the summer and then obtained light work in Coventry, but his health broke down and he was eventually admitted to the Warneford Hospital in May 1919 where he remained until he died from septic poisoning in June 1920. He was 33 years old and left a widow and son. He was given a military funeral and is buried in Kenilworth cemetery.

The Town prepares for War

Activities in Kenilworth were soon centred upon the present war crisis. News of the war's progress was sent from the Central News Agency in London both to the Conservative Club, where it was available at whatever hour it was received, and to Mr Randall, managing director of The Tannery, who posted it outside the factory. The Abbey Hill and the Church Lads' football clubs both abandoned the game for the season, sensing that to continue would not be decent. Improvement work on the parish church was stopped. As the vicar wrote in the parish magazine, 'today the stone of the sedilia are lying in a corner of the churchyard, and the masons are gone. When the storm-cloud of war burst on central Europe, we had not the heart to go on; and we need money for more urgent calls than the beautifying of the sanctuary.'

A War Relief Fund was started with donations coming from the townsfolk. The Red Cross Society very quickly got down to practical work. By the middle of August, Lady Seymour, together with her daughter Constance, was organising working parties of girls and women and 70 beds for the Red Cross were provided at Bridge House and the Parochial Hall. Practices and lectures in first aid and nursing were held practically every day under the supervision of Drs Loxton, Day and Asplen as it was expected that very soon there would be a number of wounded soldiers sent to the town for treatment. Mrs Lincoln Chandler helped set up a group of 'home workers' to make garments for soldiers and by October the first parcel of shirts had been sent to the First Southern Hospital in Birmingham.

The vicar of St Nicholas' Church, the Rev. Cairns, took over as District Commissioner of the Boy Scouts and soon had them busy making wooden bed cradles to be used to support the bed clothes on wounded soldiers' beds. He also helped set up a new rifle club at the suggestion of some of the young men in the Church Lads' Club. There was already a rifle club at St John's Church with an indoor range, which was useful for learning to shoot, but it was felt that something larger was needed where shooting at 100 yards was possible. The vicar made available a portion of glebe land in Malthouse Lane and it was lit with acetylene lamps so that it could be used in the evenings. This new rifle club was not a parochial organization but was open to any men and lads from the town who wished to join.

By October 1914, letters were arriving home from men at the front saying they did not think the war would last long. The Warwickshire Yeomanry would be shortly proceeding to the front and a call went out for Cardigan jackets, Balaclava helmets, knitted cuffs, socks, handkerchiefs, chocolates, tobacco and paper, which the townsfolk willingly provided.

The same month, a party of twenty Belgian refugees arrived in the town. Prior to their arrival a Finance and Management Committee had been formed and Bridge House (on the corner of New Street and Bridge Street) was rented and furnished for their accommodation.

The refugees were made very welcome by the people of Kenilworth. Soon after their arrival a concert at the Parochial Hall raised £15 to buy tobacco to send to Kenilworth men on active service. The Belgian refugees attended and received an ovation on entering the room.

News of the First Fatalities

In October news also began to filter through of Kenilworth men who had been killed at the front. The first was 23-year old Lance Corporal **William James Smith** who lost his life on the 15th September. As an orphan he had lived for nine years with his uncle Mr R. Biddle in Henry Street before joining the 1st Battalion Cheshire Regiment, two years before the war. His regiment had served in Ireland and he had been stabbed in the thigh during the riots in Londonderry. He has no known grave and is commemorated on La Ferté-Sous-Jouarre Memorial, Seine-et-Marne, France, along with nearly 4,000 officers and men of the British Expeditionary Force who died in August, September and early October, 1914.

In the following month, on the 19th October, only seven weeks after his marriage, Private **Henry Barnett**, known as Harry, was the first Kenilworth reservist killed in action. He was the third of Mr and Mrs Edward Barnett's five sons and had served seven years in India with the Welsh Fusiliers before entering the reserve forces in February 1913. He left for France on October 8th and his wife Amy received only one letter from him after his arrival. He told her not to worry as he would be all right and asked her to send him some cigarettes. It

Henry Barnett

was not until five weeks after his death that she received the official information from the War Office. Henry also has no known grave; his name is recorded on the Ypres (Menin Gate) Memorial, Belgium.

Three further Kenilworth privates were killed in action in October and November 1914. **Sidney Charles Aitken**, from Clinton Lane, a regular with the Coldstream Guards was killed by a shell on 23rd October. **Arthur Sawyer**, also from Clinton Lane, was with the 2nd Battalion Royal Warwickshire Regiment. He had been in the army for seven years and was stationed in Malta when war broke out and was sent from there to the front in early October. He was killed on the 7th November. **James Stanley**, a married man, also with the 2nd Battalion Royal Warwickshire Regiment, lived at Bulkington Cottages, Kenilworth and was killed at Poperinghe on the 12th November.

Meanwhile in Kenilworth life with war as a background was continuing. A new rifle range was opened in the Echo Meadow in November with members of the club (nearly 100) marching through the town from St John's Parish Rooms to the range where Major H. W. Berkeley performed the ceremony of 'breaking the flag'. The range was to be open on Tuesday and Friday evenings and Thursday and Saturday afternoons. Monday and Wednesday evenings would be devoted to route marches and drilling.

On the 14th November, *The Kenilworth Advertiser* printed a letter from **George Bricknell** of the South Staffs Regiment. George was a time-expired soldier when war broke out but immediately volunteered even though he was 34 years old and married. He lived with his wife, Emma, in Warwick Road. He was not sent over to France immediately but stayed in England for the bulk of the first twelve months as a drill instructor and very quickly gained promotion. He wrote from Borden Camp to the secretary of the Working Men's Club, to thank the members for sending cigarettes, saying:

> *We are having some rotten weather here, walking about in mud up to our knees this last week. It is still raining, with a sea-breeze travelling 80 miles an hour, and we are up most of the night trying to keep our tents up. I am pleased to tell you I have been promoted again – to corporal – through good shooting. The colonel stood behind me when I was firing and examined the target when I had finished. He turned round, and said: 'I will make you full corporal at once.' He was very pleased with my firing, a penny easily covering the five shots.*

The same edition reported that the battle in France and Flanders was continuing doggedly without any appreciable advantage either way. Mr Asquith declared in Parliament that the British casualties up to October 31st were approximately 57,000 of all ranks.

Kenilworth postman, **James Harris**, had already been involved in the fighting at Mons and wrote home to describe the realities of trench warfare, something which was to play such a major part in this war. Conditions within the trenches were often dreadful but he said that whenever it was quiet they used to make the trenches more comfortable and each relay of men improved them. They were all made big enough to allow a man to stand upright, and were cut in to allow the head and shoulders to be safeguarded from shrapnel.

At one point his battalion took up a position in a wood a few miles north of Ypres and in describing the scene he said:

> *I should call it hell upon earth. The rifle bullets whistled over the trenches. At night the bursting of the shells could be seen in every direction, and the Germans also had some kind of shell that burst a blue light which lit up everything. If we did not keep in our trenches the Germans would have been able to tell our numbers, so we had to bob down whenever they came. We were like so many rabbits bobbing up and down!*

Private Harris was injured as his regiment went to reinforce the Connaught Rangers who had lost a great many men and could no longer hold out. He was wounded by rifle bullets, one hitting his thigh and rebounding into the muscle of his arm and another hitting his forearm. He was taken to the Duchess of Westminster's Hospital at Le Touquet and after a month in hospital was sent back to England. His happiness on returning home turned to sadness when he learned that his five-year old son, Jimmie, had died from double pneumonia just a few days earlier.

Towards the end of 1914, Kenilworth's general practitioner, **Dr Reginald Tweedy**, decided he must leave his practice to help with war work and he left for Dunkirk where he was to take up the duties of a surgeon in Lady Sykes' hospital.

Shortly before Christmas 1914, a young rifleman from Kenilworth, **William Hewitt**, was killed in action. William's parents, Mr and Mrs Harry Hewitt, of Mill End, first learned of his death from the mother of his friend, Harry Cox of Henry Street. Corporal Cox had written home to his mother and asked her to inform Mr and Mrs Hewitt that their son had lost his life in an action in which they had both taken part. William Hewitt had been born in Kenilworth and, although only

ANOTHER KENILWORTH SOLDIER KILLED.

COMPANION REPORTS RIFLE-MAN HEWITT'S DEATH.

RIFLEMAN WILLIAM HEWITT.

eighteen years old, was well known throughout the town. For many years he had worked as an errand boy, although prior to joining the army he had been employed by the Dunlop Company at Coventry. He had enlisted in the 1st Battalion Rifle Brigade in March 1914 (after a year's service in the Territorials), to be with his friend Harry Cox who was already in that battalion. William was sent to France in October 1914 and joined the same company as Harry.

William wrote very few letters home and did not even let his parents know he was in the trenches until late in November. His last letter written on the 16th December 1914 expressed a desire that the war would soon end. He told his parents he was:

> ... *going on well but hoping to be able to come home, for one and all are getting sick and tired of the war. The weather out here is terrible, not a day passes without it rains and it is up to your neck in mud wherever you go. By what I hear and the way the Germans have been beaten around here I do not think the war will last long – in fact some have the idea it will not last till Xmas.*

Men of the Rifle Brigade filling sandbags for their breastworks.   *"Daily Mail" War Service*

He wished them a happy Christmas and New Year and hoped they enjoyed their turkey. On December 30th, a picture appeared on the front of the Daily Mail showing the Rifle Brigade filling sandbags ready for the fray. On the right of the photograph was William Hewitt, chilled by the winter cold as he worked with his comrades. In the foreground on the left was his pal Harry Cox. The accompanying news story told an upbeat account of the resolute British Forces preparing for the fight with the enemy.

The story was already out of date. William Hewitt and many of his comrades were killed in action on the 19th December.

When his belongings were returned to his parents they contained a letter from a young lady dated the 11th December 1914. The national press had run a campaign encouraging letters to be written to soldiers at the front. Miss Venables had obtained his name from the *Evening News* as a 'Lonely Soldier' who would appreciate the occasional letter from home. She wrote, 'I think it is simply splendid, the way you are all fighting for us, we are very proud of you.' Her two brothers and a cousin were serving but she was finding life at home very dull, 'especially at night as all the streets are so dark in preparation for a Zeppelin Invasion.' She told him she planned to send a small parcel which she hoped would help make his Christmas as merry as possible under the circumstances. She asked him if he would like anything in the way of knitting, such as socks, mittens or scarves. Her letter, spattered

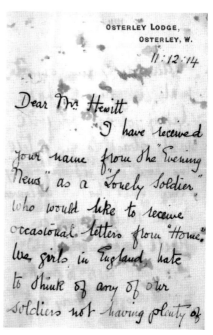

with the cold rain of the battleground, was found amongst his effects. An encouraging letter from a stranger may have been the last word he ever received from home.

William Hewitt has no known grave and his name is commemorated with those of 11,000 similar men on the Ploegsteert Memorial in Belgium. He is, however, recorded on the gravestone of his brother, Lance Corporal **Frank Hewitt**, in St Nicholas' churchyard, Kenilworth.

The headstone of Frank Hewitt with the memorial to his brother William

Frank, who served with the Royal Warwickshire Regiment, died of wounds after the war in August 1919, aged 21.

Many who died in the Great War, suffered not from injuries received on the battlefield but from the many illnesses and infectious diseases which were prevalent at the time and were largely untreatable because of the lack of medical knowledge and suitable drugs. **Edward Reeve** contracted pneumonia in camp whilst a driver with the Army Service Corps and died in Holmington Hospital, London, on the 13th September. Before the war, Edward was the 2nd whip to the North Warwickshire Huntsmen. His parents lived in Great Burstead, Essex, and he was buried in East London Cemetery at Plaistow, Essex.

Pneumonia also took the life of 18-year old **Christopher Horsley**, who died in Coventry Barracks in December 1914. Christopher was a Private in 'D' Company of the 7th (Reserve) Battalion of the Royal Warwickshire Regiment. He had lived for three years with his uncle and aunt, Mr and Mrs Upton of Albion Street, Kenilworth, his parents residing at Ratley, Edgehill. Before the outbreak of war he was employed as an under-gardener by Major Stringer in Coventry. He had joined the Territorials the previous winter and was in camp when mobilisation was ordered. Because of his young age he was transferred to the reserves and was stationed at the Coventry Barracks, where he contracted measles and later pneumonia from which he died.

His death was recognised as just as significant as those dying on the battlefield,

Christopher Horsley

and he was buried in Coventry Cemetery with a full military funeral attended by the full complement of 'D' Company, numbering about 225. The band of the Royal Munster Fusiliers played the 'Dead March' and the drums of the local battalion followed. The coffin was carried on a hearse, covered by a Union Jack, upon which lay his cap and belt. The service was conducted by the Rev. L. Richardson, chaplain of the Battalion. At the graveside the 'Last Post' was sounded, and three volleys were fired by a party from the 7th Battalion.

Christmas at Home and Abroad

Although Christmas in Kenilworth was expected to be quiet that year, entertainments were put on for the Belgian refugees and for the children of serving Kenilworth soldiers and sailors. The Belgians were treated to a fine Christmas dinner and afterwards presents were distributed to them by Mrs Percy Martin. Lord Leigh had given an 8ft high tree from his Stoneleigh estate which Mr Macartney lit with electricity. This tree was to prove the climax of the children's tea party after a conjuring entertainment and a Punch and Judy Show. On the tree was a present and a flag for each child and before they left they were each given a bag containing a mince pie, an orange and a cracker.

Christmastide 1914 in Kenilworth was a record of quietness, with not a single case of 'merriness' for the police to deal with. Decorations were missing from the shops, and, generally speaking, solemn sobriety was observed. Christmas Day opened with a glorious hoar frost, which heavily festooned the branches and twigs of the firs and for the first half of the day the countryside offered a glorious picture.

Christmas on some parts of the battle front was also surprisingly quiet. Private Alfred Smith, of the 1st Royal Warwicks, wrote to his wife on a paper serviette:

I daresay you will be surprised at me writing a letter on such paper as this, but you will be more surprised when I tell you that it contained cake given to one of our men by a German officer on Christmas Day, and I was given some of it. No doubt you will think this is a very strange proceeding, but we had not been in the trenches very long on Christmas Eve before we were shouting and wishing one another a merry Christmas. Then we invited them to come over; they did not like the idea, neither did we, of course. Some of the Germans speak English very well, so they shouted 'No shoot,' and we said the same. Then one of our sergeants went half-way to meet them, and an officer and a private came out from the German trenches. They exchanged cigarettes, and after that they sang a song and so did we. Then on Christmas morning we all went out of the trenches and met the Germans half-way. We were able to bury our dead, some of whom had been lying there for six weeks or more. We are still on speaking terms with them, so that we have not fired a shot at them up to now (December 29th), neither have they, so that the snipers on each side have had a rest.

In spite of the lull in the fighting and this extraordinary fraternisation between the enemies, the war was not over by Christmas as many had predicted. Eight Kenilworth men had lost their lives since the outbreak in August, having all volunteered willingly to defend their country. The town had embraced with gusto all the different activities in aid of the war effort and at the end of 1914 there was still optimism that the war would be short-lived

THE KENILWORTH ADVERTISER, DECEMBER 26, 1914.

when your country is in danger.

The Post of Honour is in the Firing Line.
Enlist to-day, and become fit to fight for England, Home and Duty.

Chapter 3

1915 – Realisation

Early in the new year the first Zeppelin raid on mainland Britain took place. On the night of the 19th January bombs were dropped from the German airship over Great Yarmouth and King's Lynn killing five people. The war had now become one of 'total war' involving warfare on land, sea and from the air.

On the Western Front the stalemate continued and conditions in the trenches were dreadful, yet the spirit amongst the Kenilworth soldiers remained high. They wrote home to thank people for the Christmas gifts purchased out of the proceeds of the Tobacco Fund Concert. Trooper J. Carter was pleased to know that they were not forgotten:

> *I must say the people at home are doing their share in this war by the splendid way they are looking after us boys at the front. We are getting well provided with war clothing and various other comforts, but I can assure you we want it, for the weather here is awful, and soon ruins the best of things. .... The last lot of trenches we were in were a foot deep with water and mud, and to have to stick three days and nights in that, and a man to every yard of trench, is no joke. Still we keep smiling, for we know the Huns are worse off then we are.*

Many of Kenilworth's recruits to Kitchener's Army had spent Christmas at home and those who had been in training since August were expecting to go abroad shortly. The majority were enjoying their training and when interviewed by the local paper, made comments such as, 'Not overworked', 'Well fed', 'Never felt better'; it was noted that there had been an all-round improvement in their physical

Troops at training camp

appearance. The spirit of this 'New Army' was buoyant and all were keen to 'do their bit'. One recruit commented: 'We'll make the Germans sit up for it. They will get such a surprise when Kitchener's Army goes out, for every one is thoroughly efficient, so they must look out for squalls. We are told to hold ourselves in readiness to go any moment. For myself I am anxious to go just to do my whack.'

More and more men were being needed at the front, and Lord Kitchener was endeavouring to obtain these without having to bring in conscription. Over 300 men had been recruited from Kenilworth, but it was felt that there was still a large number of able-bodied, eligible young men who should be fighting for their country. On the 12th of January a recruiting meeting was held at the Abbey Hotel assembly room to encourage these men to come forward. Stirring addresses were made by Mr A. W. Street, chairman of the town council, and Mr Alfred Bigland, MP, putting forward arguments why more men should join up; if more men went, then the sooner the war would be over, but it was also a duty and privilege for men to fight for their rights as Britishers and to act as avengers of the atrocities the Germans had committed in Belgium. Above all, the speakers appealed to the men's consciences describing the gulf that would inevitably appear between those that went and those that did not. Captain Kay, recruiting officer for the district, urged the men to 'shoulder your responsibilities, and the more quickly get this thing behind us.'

Kenilworth's general practitioner, **Dr Tweedy**, had been taking his duty seriously and had just arrived home from France after six weeks' work at Lady Sykes' hospital. This was a British hospital for French wounded at Dunkirk accommodating 40 patients and staffed by two surgeons, a house-surgeon and 13 nurses. They treated seriously wounded patients, most of whom were operation cases. Hospital trains came in twice daily on an average, in the morning and early evening. The doctors, with their stretcher-bearers, met the trains, and when they had vacant beds chose their patients. When conditions allowed, wounds were dressed in the evening on arrival and, after a night's rest, the operations took place next day. Very often, urgent cases kept the operating surgeons busy all through the night. There were six hospitals in Dunkirk in two enormous goods sheds, one of which held 300 beds. On one day, when the Germans were trying to break through to Calais, 3000 wounded were brought back for treatment.

Private **James Harris,** the former postman, fully recovered from his wounds by the end of January, returned to his depot at Lichfield. Before he left, the staff at the Kenilworth Post Office had subscribed together to buy him a cardigan jacket, two pairs of mittens, a muffler, tobacco and a pipe. Miss Young, the postmistress, made the presentation, dwelling on Lord Kitchener's words of advice to the army that the peace of the world would be unsettled if the war was not fought to a finish. She wished Private Harris, on behalf of the staff, all luck and a safe return. Before leaving, Private Harris handed each of the staff a copy of a recent photograph of himself as a memento of the occasion.

The Red Cross Hospital

In February 1915, the recently-built Parochial Hall was converted into the Kenilworth Red Cross Hospital for the treatment of wounded soldiers and opened for the first party of nineteen patients who arrived by train from the First Southern Hospital at Birmingham. None of these were really serious cases—most were suffering from frost-bitten feet. The hall was fitted out thanks to the generosity of the townspeople, although three days previously, when notice of these wounded soldiers was received, the hall was being used as a soldiers' club and had in no

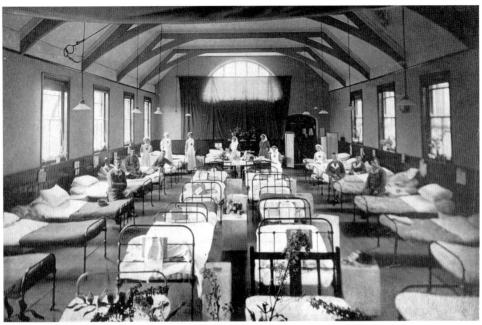

The Red Cross Hospital in the Parochial Hall

way been prepared. The local Red Cross Society, under its commandant, Dr Asplen, soon had it scrubbed and thoroughly cleansed. Beds were fetched from those who had promised to lend them, a bathroom was hurriedly constructed and within three days the place was transformed into a hospital. The hall, which was large and airy, was used for a ward. The bathroom had a constant supply of hot water from a geyser which had been fitted, and the front room was turned into a smoking and recreation room, in which there was a piano and a gramophone. The accommodation was comfortably able to hold 40 patients and, to help provide fresh food for these recovering soldiers, a 'Pound Day' was held every Saturday at the caretaker's home in nearby Stanley House, when household goods of all kinds were received, with fresh eggs and green vegetables particularly welcomed.

Towards the end of January, Lance Sergeant Gilbert Liggins was expected home on leave. He was one of the sons of Joseph Liggins an old-established Kenilworth baker with premises in Stoneleigh Road. Gilbert had been a regular soldier for nine years and re-enlisted in the 16th Lancers in August 1914 for a further twelve. He was promoted during the war from corporal to sergeant and, as one of the finest horsemen in his regiment, had been selected to ride at Olympia.

His wife waited patiently until March when she received an official notice that he had been missing since the 21st February. It transpired that the 16th Lancers had joined the French lines in the early days of the Yser operations but, on arrival, had been blown up in the trenches, burying most of the occupants. Gilbert's fate was uncertain, but it was hoped he might have survived and been rescued or captured.

Trooper J. Carter, of the 9th Lancers, who was invalided home, reported that his regiment had relieved the 16th Lancers after their trenches had been blown in, and he feared that Sergeant Liggins was amongst the missing. Sergeant H. Satchwell also sent home

CORPORAL GILBERT LIGGINS MISSING.

BURIED WHILST HELPING OUR ALLIES.

CORPORAL LIGGINS.

word to the same effect, so that there seemed little hope, although there was a possibility that he had been taken prisoner by the Germans. Neither the British War Office nor the German Concentration Camps had any news of him. When Sergeant Satchwell returned to Kenilworth on leave in August, he reported to Gilbert's family that he had made searching inquiries for news of him but, from accounts received from the missing man's chums, he was forced to conclude that Sergeant Liggins was numbered amidst the slain. No trace was ever found of him and his name is recorded on the Ypres (Menin Gate) Memorial.

Soldiers come to town

During February 1915, the town hosted 400 members of the Army Service Corps. These men, who were mostly from the Winchester and Andover area, were billeted with the townspeople before their departure for France. They were made to feel very welcome. The castle was thrown open, the churches gave them access to their buildings, and local clubs and institutes allowed them to join without payment. Their parades and drilling, which took place around the area of The Square, proved to be of great interest to the local people.

The following month the 1st Battalion Royal Dublin Fusiliers stayed for nine days before leaving for an unknown destination. They found a special place in the hearts of Kenilworth people. Not only did they look like a magnificent fighting battalion as they marched into Kenilworth, but they also proved to be good company in the homes where they were billeted, being full of humour and ever ready with a laugh. Nevertheless, not all approved of the soldiers' presence in the town. The vicar of St Nicholas' church, although admitting that the soldiers behaved extremely well, commented in the church magazine on the behaviour of a few of the 'less steady young people' and added that 'It is not a pleasant sight to see your women deliberately trying to attract the attention of the soldiers.'

After their stay the men went off with songs and roars of laughter through the ranks. *The Kenilworth Advertiser* reported that:

.... one can conceive them still laughing, and making light of the hard times in front of them. The Dublins have a score to wipe off, and if

The Dublin Fusiliers marching along Warwick Rd

their destination is other than France they will be keenly disappointed. They feel that the regiment's grand record has to be added to at the Germans' expense after the cutting up of the 2nd Battalion in the dark days of the Mons retreat. Anyone seeing them at their drill, or on their long route marches under their heavy equipment, could not fail to be impressed with their quality.

On the 12th of March they paraded out of town to assemble with a massed force of 18,000 men and 6,000 horses at Ryton on Dunsmore where the ancient Fosse Way crosses Thomas Telford's historic road from London to Holyhead. There they were reviewed by King George V before a crowd some seven to ten thousand strong and sent on their way to fight at an unknown destination.

The Dubliners' stay in the town created a boom in trade, particularly with the tobacconists who were practically cleared out of their stock as people bought heavily to make parting gifts.

They were sent to battle not in France, as they had hoped, but in the Dardanelles as part of the Gallipoli campaign. Their fate was not victory but a fierce encounter in which over half of the rank and file were injured and only two out of 28 officers came through unscathed. Six of their number were burned alive.

King George inspecting his troops at Dunsmore

Gallipoli and the Middle East

The Gallipoli campaign was one of the worst disasters suffered by the Allies in the war. It had been an attempt to knock Turkey out of the war by naval action. When the first two phases of the expedition failed to do this, a land expedition was mounted, which put ashore on the 25th April. By this time, Turkish defences had been substantially strengthened, with the result that the combined force of British, French, Australian and New Zealand troops found themselves pinned down between the sea and hills held by the Turks. A landing of fresh troops on the 6th August made little difference and by November 1915 total failure was admitted and the survivors were evacuated.

Four local men died in the Gallipoli campaign, all during the month of August. Private **John Cashmore** was with the 9th Battalion, Royal Warwickshire Regiment, whilst Private **John Weyman,** a married man from Hammond's Terrace, Clinton Lane and Second Lieutenant **Sidney Butler**, from Lower Ladyes Hills, were both serving with the Welsh Fusiliers. **Oswald Winstanley** was reported missing on the 10th August. He was 27 and had joined the Warwickshire Regiment as a volunteer in November 1914, leaving his father's gas engineering firm, Messrs. G. Winstanley & Sons. The family lived at Crackley Hall and was very well known within the town for taking part in concerts and amateur theatrical performances in aid of deserving local causes. Oliver received a commission with the 5th Welsh Regiment in February 1915 and sailed from England on the 18th July. No further news was received of him and his mother died eighteen months later not knowing his fate. It was eventually concluded that he had been killed on the day he was reported missing.

These men's names are on the Helles Memorial in Turkey amongst 20,000 others whose graves are unknown or who were lost or buried at sea off Gallipoli.

Private **Bert Faxon**, of School Lane, was also involved in fighting the Turks in the spring of 1915, not in the Dardanelles but with the Royal Field Artillery in Persia. He wrote home to his parents:

> *You will be surprised to hear I am not in England, but in the supposed Garden of Eden, encamped at a place called Gurna, on the banks of the River Tigris. We have not been doing any fighting for the last few days, but I don't suppose the Turks will let us rest for long. We do not*

mind how often they come in the daytime, but the Turks like fighting at night, and try to surprise us asleep; but we are not so easily caught as that, and they get a 'towsing' every time. After arriving here from India, we were in action next day, but the battle only lasted the one day. We saw some dreadful sights, but our killed and wounded only amounted to 300, whereas the losses of the enemy totalled about 1,700. After a rest of a couple of weeks we had a big battle which lasted three days. I am getting used to sleeping on the ground – have got corns on my back from it.

Bert was to die the following year, a couple of months after being taken prisoner when he was with the ill-fated division under General Townshend at Kut-al-Almara. The failure of the Gallipoli campaign ensured the continuation of the war in France and Flanders.

Further Losses in France

Sam Insall of Whitemoor, aged nineteen, was killed in action at Festubert on Easter Monday, 6th April. He was shot through the heart. The news of Sam's death was sent home via a Coventry chum who had joined up with him at the outbreak of hostilities. Private Insall had already served three years in the 3rd Reserve Battalion of the Oxford and Bucks Light Infantry, joining up for training two months in each year. He was called up in August 1914, and was highly elated at the prospect of seeing active service. *The Kenilworth Advertiser* described him as 'a bright youth of a daring disposition, and one who would make a good soldier.'

Sam Insall

He went to France early in December 1914 to serve in the trenches and had two short spells in hospital; he was discharged on the 28th March 1915 after illness. In a letter to his parents he wrote:

We are getting some nice weather out here now, and about time, for it has been nothing but rain up till recently, and we have had to go up to the trenches waist deep at times. I cannot tell you where we are, but there has been some scrapping. You should just hear the artillery when they start chucking old iron at one another.

His chum wrote to his father in Coventry asking him to break the news to Private Insall's parents, and mentioned that he had seen the grave in which Sam had been laid to rest.

At the Second Battle of Ypres in April 1915, Private **Frederick Bayliss** of Mill End was reported missing and Private **William Wilkshire** of Bridge Street was killed. Both were with the 1st Battalion, Royal Warwickshire Regiment. This battle encompassed four engagements in the northern sector of the Ypres Salient, the first beginning on the 22nd April as a surprise offensive by the German 4th Army on the Allied front line. It also saw the introduction of a new German weapon with the use of poisonous gas for the first time in the history of warfare.

Springtime in Kenilworth

Back in Kenilworth, the life of the town was slowly changing in the face of the war effort. By the spring of 1915 the Tannery was working at full stretch to produce leather for army boots. Since the war started, it had delivered three million pounds of leather which contributed in large part to the 3,700,000 pairs of boots purchased by the Government for the war effort and many thousands of pairs continued to be required weekly. Work at the Kenilworth Skin Works was also very brisk with the wool produced being sent to Yorkshire where nearly all of it was required for Army purposes, particularly khaki goods.

Three Belgian refugees at Bridge House

Kenilworth employers were finding difficulty in obtaining labour since practically all those who were eligible had joined the Colours and those who remained often preferred to seek employment in Coventry where the rates of pay had increased.

More Belgian refugees arrived to stay at Bridge House in April, this time there were three women, two from Brussels and one from Antwerp, who told the local press about the conditions in Belgium, particularly in Brussels, where the Germans had established an iron rule. Although life in the city was generally quiet and monotonous the population were made to pay heavily for everything they obtained from the Germans. A rigid press censorship had been imposed and anyone caught with an English paper was severely punished. Even so, copies of *The Times* and *The Daily Telegraph* were regularly smuggled in and eagerly read.

Kenilworth Volunteer Training Corps and Rifle Club

Throughout England men were now banding together to form volunteer training corps, particularly men who were too old to be soldiers or could not leave their businesses. Some months before it had been decided to form a county regiment with Colonel Wyley as its first commandant, and to map out the county into battalions. Kenilworth had its own Volunteer Training Corps and Rifle Club, and in March 1915, Lincoln Chandler wrote to the press expressing his feelings that it should be properly organised. He complained that it now consisted

" Herald " Photo.

Back row (standing), left to right : Messrs. G. F. Powell, C. Hetherington, Sholto Douglas, L. W. Pratt, J. A. Jordan, F. Elstub, F. H. Hope, S. Wells.
Second row (kneeling): Messrs. E. S. Barnett, A. Roberts, D. W. Wilkie (sergeant), W. R. Shingler (quartermaster), E. J. Johnson.
Front row (prone): Messrs. B. K. Lewis, O. Beck (Co.-Sergt.-Major), R. Gabb, H. E. Watson, —. Sandy (armourer-sergt.), G. Harwood.

Kenilworth Training Corps at Rifle Practice

of 20 to 30 youths entirely from the working classes and about half a dozen 'crocks' like himself. They had no Commanding Officer and he felt 'people who should be interested did not appear to care a damn about the Corps.' He called for a public meeting to settle the question of the Corps, concluding 'either end it or mend it.'

Mr Chandler's words obviously struck home as a public meeting was arranged two weeks later for the purpose of reconstituting the Corps. Kenilworth already had an excellent rifle range, as one of the most important things was to train men to shoot and now, in addition, the men would be expected to do a certain amount of drill to raise their efficiency, in case of a possible invasion.

In the fortnight after the public meeting membership of the volunteer corps doubled and the committee planned to canvass all the eligible men in the town to increase numbers further. It was also decided to separate the boys from the men in the marches and drilling, because, with the difference of twenty years in the ages of those eligible to join, there was a sort of mixing of the 'sublime and ridiculous' (as the local paper reported it so aptly), which tended to retard recruiting. Mr J. H. Bates, whose son Harold had joined the army as a volunteer, was made platoon commander.

The War spreads to London

In May, London witnessed its first attack from the air as bombs were dropped from Zeppelin airships and the same month news was received of the terrible *Lusitania* disaster. The British liner, on her way from New York to Liverpool, was sunk by the Germans with the loss of over 1000 lives. Mr and Mrs Hopkins of Henry Street lost two daughters, Alice and Kate, who were coming home from America for a sister's wedding. Also the Tomms family, who used to work for the Amhersts of Fieldgate, lost one of their daughters, Lizzie. She was on her way from Canada to Erdington to nurse her invalid mother.

The Kenilworth Red Cross Hospital was filled to capacity at this time after a rush of patients from the Southern Hospital at Birmingham where more serious cases were arriving from Ypres. Most of these were wounded and invalided cases, none of them yet suffering from the effects of the German gas. Lady Seymour made a plea for more people to come forward to increase the hospital staff, particularly men for the men's section.

At the front, several Kenilworth men were being treated in hospital. Rifleman A. Tebby, of Spring Lane, who was with the King's Royal Rifles, had been put out of action after only about a week's fighting. In a letter to his wife he made light of his injuries:

> *Bar my wounds I am in the best of health. I got shrapnel wounds in the left leg, left arm, and left hand, and except for the shrapnel in the arm all the pieces have been removed, but I shall have to have an operation for the removal of the piece in the arm. I got the wounds in the trenches. You can see more here now in a day than in six weeks when the weather was bad. We had a 'rough house' for about twelve hours, and they levelled the trenches, but we shall beat them in time. I have seen Drane, Fred Puffet, and Harry Cox and have been close to Heath and young Vic Gardner, but could not get in touch with them.* [These were all Kenilworth men.]

A Kenilworth man was one of the first to be gassed by the Germans. Private H. Garrett, of Lion Yard, who was with the Royal Warwickshires had seen some hard fighting. In a letter to his wife he wrote:

> *I could fill a book with what we have been through this last week or so, but to cut it short, the longest day of my life was a week last Sunday. We were to take a trench, a wood, and a village (where don't matter). We marched all day and night, and it rained like hell. Halt forty minutes on the side of the road, then again trekked on until we got to where we were to open out from. We got going, and over came their lights. ... My word it grew hot; we were only 80 yards from their trenches when we had the order to retire, as the Germans could have wiped us clean out. We lost quite enough as it was, and I was one of the lucky ones to get back without a scratch. It was last Sunday afternoon that I got my dose of gas – the devils dropped their stinkers right on top of us. It was an unpleasant quarter of an hour I had – just a race for life, but I'm here all right, and if I get back up there then I'll kill everyone I get near. I have not forgotten our chaps on that field. Everyone of our men are of the same mind, and when we get near them, Lord help them; it will be a case of get out or get under.*

Whilst the Kenilworth soldiers were having a busy time in and out of the trenches, life was proving rather monotonous for some of those in the Royal Navy. When Stoker **Ernest Ashmore** paid a flying visit to his home in Spring Lane, Kenilworth, in June 1915, he gave the reporter of the *Coventry Herald* a glimpse into the work of the torpedo boat destroyers which were constantly conveying troops to the shores of France. He said he would prefer a 'scrap' now and again just to enliven the monotony and added that they never expected to see a German ship now, although if one did come they would be prepared to give it a warm welcome. He had previously been in the submarine service and was expecting to be recalled to that branch of the Navy very soon.

Women and Children play their part

As summer approached, with more and more men joining the forces, their places at home were taken by women and girls. Nationally they joined the newly-formed women's police force and worked on trains and buses. In the factories they took a major part in the war effort. Three million women were employed making shells, the largest contingent being at the Woolwich Arsenal. Large numbers were also working the land, sharing the effort with the men who remained to do the heaviest work.

In Kenilworth, children in the local schools were being kept busy playing their part in serving their country. Sandbags were wanted

Kenilworth Messenger girls

by the million at the front, so the County Education Committee had recommended to headteachers the making of sandbags. As sewing was part of the routine work, it was thought a good idea to utilise the children's service in a practical way and also enable the children to 'do their bit.' Mr A. Hacking, headmaster of St Nicholas' school, sent off a batch of 92 bags as a first contribution from his scholars.

With so many of the local postmen having joined the army, three young Kenilworth girls, Alice Reeve, Beatrice Peck and Edith Aitken, became telegraph messengers.

Throughout June, Kenilworth experienced a long spell of hot weather. There was a record attendance at the baths in the first three weeks of the month and several schools took their pupils each week to teach them to swim. It was forecast that the strawberry season would be a short one because of the drought, but the fruit trees and bushes promised heavy crops. The drought ended at the beginning of July with half an inch of rain falling one night.

The weather was also very hot in France and Ursula Graves, of Waverley House, Kenilworth, wife of Lieutenant Graves, Medical Officer with the 8th Royal Warwicks Regiment, wrote to *The Kenilworth Advertiser* asking local people to help supply socks and shirts:

> *My husband tells me that the men are suffering from the effects of the long route marchs in the hot, dusty weather, and many of them have bad feet from wearing old ragged socks. The men will shortly be going to the front, and the officers are working very hard to get them fit. It seems a pity that any lack that we might support should hinder their efficiency.*

During the hot summer of 1915, the picturesque cottages at Little Virginia, Kenilworth were acquired by Mr Lincoln Chandler. He intended to preserve them in an old-world style by re-thatching and refurbishing those that could be repaired, whilst others were to be demolished and the old stone used for facing the remaining buildings. The designs for the rebuilt cottages were described as extremely pretty with large windows and thatched roofs.

The Kenilworth Advertiser commented that Kenilworth was indebted to Mr Chandler for saving this property from the speculative builders' hands, maintaining Little Virginia in all its old-world quaintness, and in keeping with the old cottages facing the castle gates.

Cottages in Little Virginia

King George passes through Kenilworth

Mr Chandler was also able to please the Kenilworth townsfolk in July by arranging for the Royal train to slow down as it came through the railway station. He had had the honour of lunching with the King the previous week in Coventry and said how delighted the wounded soldiers at the Kenilworth Red Cross Hospital would be for an opportunity of seeing his Majesty as he passed through the railway station on his return journey. King George readily agreed and personally ordered the Royal train to slow down.

On the day, Mr Chandler arranged for the soldiers and part of the nursing staff to be transported to the railway station; as the Royal train came in, it slowed to no more than a slow walking pace. The King was at a doorway, the window of which was wide open, and he stood at the salute whilst passing the assembled soldiers, who gave him a rousing cheer.

Amongst the soldier patients assembled were three who had been inspected by the King at Dunsmore in March, and who had since seen action in the Dardanelles where they were injured.

The patients at the Red Cross Hospital were extremely grateful for all the care they received in Kenilworth and one of them, Private C.

Holt, expressed his gratitude by composing a poem,

This is the home to come to, boys –
A home you will all admire;
For you are treated as a soldier:
Yes, even like a Squire.

The sisters and nurses love you
As if you were their own.
And they treat you, lads, with tender care,
Like poor mother did at home.

And when our task is over,
As on our way we roam,
Just offer up a prayer, lads,
For blessings for the staff of this home.

Letters from the Front

Whilst local residents enjoyed the long hot summer, news from the war was getting worse. Private **James Harris**, the Kenilworth postman, was back in the trenches. He wrote to his fellow colleagues thanking them for gifts of tobacco and said:

The position of the lines we are holding now is very dangerous as we are only 25 yards from the Germans, and we exchange bombs all day and night. I am sorry to say we had thirty casualties, three killed and twenty-seven wounded in the four days we were in the trenches. The ground between us is undermined by both sides, and we blew up one of the German trenches the other day and killed fifteen and buried twenty-five in the debris, so you see we are playing them at their own game. I am glad to see that their sap heads and mines are not so accurate as ours, for ours did twice the amount of damage.

At sea in July, Lord Seymour's youngest son, Lieutenant Commander Arthur Seymour was wounded on a gunboat in the Euphrates River. He survived the war but six Kenilworth men died in the month of August, the four already mentioned who died at Gallipoli and two who were in France, **Harry Cox** and **Harold Bates**.

Sergeant **Harry Cox**, the pal of William Hewitt, died in August from wounds received in action in July. He had joined the Army in August 1913 and went to France as a rifleman with the 1st Battalion

Sergeant Harry Cox

Rifle Brigade on September 19th, 1914. In July 1915, his mother, Mrs Cox of 89 Henry Street, received a postcard from a Sheffield hospital to say that her son had been wounded by an explosive bullet in the thigh in an engagement in La Bassée district on the 6th of July.

Since arriving in France, Sergeant Cox had been continually at the front. During this time, although only aged 20, he was promoted to Corporal in December, awarded his sergeant's stripes in May, and had been recommended for quartermaster-sergeant when he was injured.

He was very popular in his regiment, and one of the wounded soldiers who was staying at the Kenilworth Red Cross Hospital called on his mother to tell her how much her son was admired by his colleagues. He said he distinguished himself in every battle and was always picked out by his Colonel when any special work wanted doing.

Harry kept a diary which gave the following version of how he was wounded and the subsequent events:

Made an attack on July 6th, and got wounded: shot through and broken thigh bone. Lay in trench from 5.30 a.m. to 11.30 p.m. Carried to dressing station two miles away. Got into ambulance at Pepperherge. Early next morning had an operation. Next day again put into ambulance, and arrived at Etaples late in the night. Had another operation next day. Stopped there until the 11th; was booked for England, and set sail on the 12th. Arrived at Sheffield 10.30 p.m. the same day. In bed ever since.

His mother was with him in Sheffield for a fortnight and said he was wonderfully bright and cheerful. His death was wholly unexpected. An operation to remove his leg took place but Harry died from shock three hours later, collapsing after regaining consciousness. His body was brought back to Kenilworth and he was given a full military funeral at St Nicholas' parish church, the first to be performed in the town. Forty members of the Kenilworth Volunteer Training Corps under Acting-Captain Lincoln Chandler and Sergeants Beck and Barnwell attended and stood at salute as the coffin was borne into the church.

Shortly after Harry Cox's death, Kenilworth lost one of its young commissioned officers. Twenty-four year old Lieutenant **Harold Christopher Bates,** the son of the Platoon Commander of the Kenilworth Voluntary Training Corps, was reported killed 'in a storm of bullets' while working on fortifications. Harold was promoted to Lieutenant after a period of training at Chatham and Bulford, and left for France on the 18th July 1915. He died a month later on the 20th of August. The circumstances of his death were sent in a letter to his parents by Major Butterworth:

Lieutenant Harold Bates

No. 3 (Harold's) section were putting up a wire entanglement round a small work called Colom Post, some little way (150 yards, perhaps) behind the firing line. They started work at about 9 p.m., and all went well until 11 p.m. A few bullets passed from time to time, but it was comparatively quiet. Just at 11, a machine gun opened fire from a point to the right of the post, which was replied to by the enemy by heavy machine gun and rifle fire. A storm of bullets swept over the work, and one of these hit poor Harold in the forehead. He went down without a sound, and death must have been quite (or nearly) instantaneous. Sergeant Barraclough and Corporal Hider were with him, and not knowing the extent of his injuries they dressed the wound and took him with all speed to the aid-post of the 1st Seaforths. Here I found him at midnight with four of his section in attendance. Nothing could be done. It was a dreadful blow, as I hoped all along that things were not so bad. I was in the billet, and the message to me was that he was wounded. We carried him back to the place where the section waggons were packed, and then brought him back here. His section behaved splendidly. They all loved him to a man, and his loss to the section and the company is greater than I can estimate. Personally, I mourn for a dear friend, for his lovable disposition, cheerfulness and keenness for his work, had endeared him to myself and the entire company. Ever since we came up here and have been under fire, he has been an example to everyone of pluck and general courage. I never saw him once flinch and duck at a bullet, which very few can say at the start.

Award for Gallantry

News reached the town in August of the award
of a Distinguished Conduct Medal (DCM) to a
Kenilworth man for the first time in this war. It
was won by 22-year old Lance-Corporal Leonard
Henry Reeve of Warwick Road, Kenilworth.

Leonard Henry, known locally as Billy and
often referred to in the local press as William
Reeve, had as a youth been a good shot in the
St John's Air Rifle Club. When he joined the 1st
King's Royal Rifles in August 1914, he was soon
amongst the 'crackshots' being sent out to the
front in November.

Lance-Corporal 'Billy' Reeve

He was in the trenches throughout the winter but did not see much
action until the spring. His battalion was at Givenchy on March 10th,
and attacked the Germans simultaneously with the British advance at
Neuve Chappelle. A severe bombardment opened at 6.30 a.m., and the
infantry attack was launched at 8 a.m.

Reeve's battalion was the only one in the neighbourhood of
Givenchy to gain a footing in the German trenches, and only 15 of their
men penetrated the enemy's lines. They found just four unwounded
Germans in the section of trench they entered and, splitting into three
parties, they proceeded to set up barricades on either side of them
and across the communication trench linking to the German reserve
trenches.

Lance-Corporal Reeve was with a private in the communication
trench and they held out for six hours, killing three Germans right
close up to their barricade, before they were eventually driven back
by bombs. The other parties were similarly repulsed, and their
Captain, who had been twice wounded and was helpless, realised the
hopelessness of staying there unsupported, and ordered his men back.
Only four of them reached the British lines.

Reeve was crawling back when a wounded rifleman from his
battalion asked him to take him along. Getting him on his back,
Corporal Reeve proceeded to crawl away and, as events proved, his
valiant action proved to be the means of his own salvation. The soldier
on his back survived, but he also acted as a shield and was hit several
times while Corporal Reeve was wounded in the back of the head. For

his heroism, his commanding officer, Major Shakerley, recommended
him for the Distinguished Conduct Medal.

After a month in hospital Corporal Reeve rejoined his battalion
who were then supporting the 1st Division attack at Festubert. Major
Shakerley was killed in this action and Corporal Reeve got a bullet in
his thigh and was in hospital until July. He was presented with his DCM
by Lord Hardinge, Commandant of the Rifle Depot at Winchester, on
Wednesday, August 4th.

Following the news of the presentation of the DCM, the Kenilworth
Urban District Council offered their congratulations and approved a
suggestion by the Chairman, Mr A. W. Street and Vice-Chairman, Dr
W. Growse, that a testimonial be made to Corporal Reeve whereby
subscriptions (which would be limited to one shilling) would be
received by Mr A. E. Dencer of Bridge Street. The idea was not to obtain
a large sum of money, but rather to get a long list of Kenilworth people
willing to show their appreciation of the young man's gallantry. The
plan was to make a presentation to him when he next came home on
leave.

There was a temporary respite from thinking about the war when the
Mop Fair was held at the end of September, beginning on a Saturday
night in a field off the Warwick Road and continuing on the following
Monday and Tuesday. The interlude did not last long as news was
received of further deaths.

Sergeant **Albert E. Overton** from Henry Street and Private **Frank
Sabin**, who were both with the 2nd Battalion Royal Warwickshire
Regiment, were killed on the 25th September, the first day of the British
advance at Loos. Private **Donald Ewen** of the London Regiment, was
killed by a sniper in the same battle on 16th October.

It was at the battle of Loos that the British used gas on the Germans
for the first time, but this was not entirely successful. In places the
wind blew it back into the British trenches, resulting in many British
casualties, although only seven actually died.

Meanwhile, at a hospital in Eastbourne, 18-year old Bombardier
Laurie Seekings, one of five brothers from Barrowell Terrace, (now
Borrowell) Kenilworth, died on the 28th September from an illness
brought on by wounds received in action.

Bombardier Seekings had enlisted under age before the war when
he was only sixteen and served two years in the Royal Field Artillery.

Bombardier Laurie Seekings

He went out to France with his Battery early in August 1914 and fought through the early stages of the war, at Mons, Neuve Chapelle, and later at La Bassée, where he received the wounds which accelerated his death.

By the autumn of 1915, life became increasingly busy in Kenilworth. As more soldiers were wounded at the front, the patients at the Red Cross Hospital had increased to 29 and the distributing hospital (Holymoor, Birmingham) was making enquiries about a possible increase in accommodation. Six more beds were immediately brought in (making a total of 35), and every bed was expected to be occupied within a day or two. It was also proposed to erect a temporary building on ground to the rear of the Parochial Hall to be used for open-air recreation or, if absolutely necessary, an open-air ward. This would cost £150 and an appeal was put out for funds.

The Vicar of St Nicholas', the Rev. Cairns, also organised an appeal. He had been in touch with a new organization called the A.O.V. (Amateur Ordnance Volunteers) and sought help from anyone who could do a little metal lathe work and who either had, or had access to, a lathe. He intended to make shell bases, many thousands of which had already been made successfully by amateurs. He also planned to start carpentry classes for ladies to make bed-tables for wounded soldiers in hospital.

The Kenilworth Volunteer Training Corps was busy practically every day of the week with drill and rifle practice. A new indoor range had been opened at Hawkes' brickworks and was used twice a week, whilst Saturdays and Sundays were often spent on the service range in Stoneleigh Park.

At the beginning of November it was decided that some public lighting should be resumed in the town in spite of the threat of Zeppelins and 18 out of 176 street lamps would remain alight. These would be ones at most of the street corners although the tops of the lamps were blackened in readiness for any action. It was also decided, for the sake of economy, to start the afternoon session at the schools half an hour earlier in order to save coal and gas. This would also mean the children would be able to get home safely before darkness set in when the streets were only partially lit.

Former postman, Private **James Harris**, wrote a letter to his wife in Henry Street on the 15th November 1915 revealing his feelings at still being in the trenches. 'Just a few lines to you to let you know that I am going on all right .... We are in the trenches again for a few days and it is very cold and damp, but never mind, we must be satisfied with being alive and pretty fair in health, only for a cold.' He also asked her to pass on a parody of the well-known song 'Sing Me to Sleep' to the *Coventry Herald*, which was adapted by individual soldiers to suit their own circumstances. This was Private Harris's version:

Sing me to sleep, where bullets fall,
Let me forget the war and all.
Damp is my dug-out, cold are my feet,
Nothing but bully and biscuits to eat.
Sing me to sleep where bombs explode,
And shrapnel shells are à la mode.
Over the sandbags helmets you find,
Corpses in front of you, corpses behind.

Far from the trenches I long to be,
Where German snipers can't pot at me.
Think of me crouching where worms do creep,
Waiting for someone to put me to sleep.
Sing me to sleep in some old shed,
A dozen rat holes around my head,
Stretched out along on my waterproof,
And dodging the raindrops from the roof.

Sing me to sleep where camp fires glow,
For over the top we've got to go.
Dreaming of home and nights in the West.

Somebody's boots resting on my chest.
Far from Henry Street I seem to be,
Lights of old Kenilworth I'd rather see:
Think of me crouching where worms do creep,
Waiting for sergeant to say 'Next relief!'

Later in the month he wrote to his Post Office colleagues vividly describing his life in the trenches:

We have been very busy but I am pleased to say that I pulled through safely, although I had some narrow escapes when we were charging and taking the German trenches. My comrades on left and right fell, and it makes one think to see them fall. We found plenty of German dead and wounded lying about when we got their trenches. The Germans tried their utmost to recover the lost trenches, but we repulsed them every time with heavy losses. They started using the gas and liquid fire, and I got gassed slightly, but nothing dangerous, as I did not get enough of it, for I held my breath till I got my gas helmet on. The gas turned our buttons and badges green, and we held on until reinforced.

News came at the beginning of November of a further soldier's death and with it widespread regret was felt throughout the town.

Second-Lieutenant Cuthbert Allen

Second-Lieutenant **Cuthbert G. L. Allen**, the younger son of the Rev. C. Llewellyn Allen, the minister at Abbey Hill Congregational Church, died from wounds received in France.

Second-Lieutenant Allen, who was 32 and single, had emigrated to South Africa in 1906 and was employed for some time as a bank clerk. He subsequently studied surveying and obtained a good post as a mining surveyor at a Krugersdorp Gold Mine.

When war broke out he joined the South African forces and served throughout General Botha's successful campaign against German South-West Africa. When the South African force was disbanded he returned to England in

August 1915 with the object of enlisting in the British forces in Europe. In September he received a commission in the Royal Engineers and two weeks later went to France.

The letters sent home by Cuthbert since leaving England shone with his spirit of determination through heavy fighting. In one dated September 26th, very shortly after his arrival in France, he wrote, 'We had a very exciting day yesterday. One of our officers who was with me said that it was the most terrible action he has been in, and he has been out here for nine months.'

A further letter stated that having finished his ordinary duties early in the day, he got permission from his commanding officer to assist in an infantry attack by another branch of the Army and so was able to see a good deal of the fighting. 'I was surprised to find', he said, 'that shells bursting around me did not damp my spirits, though once or twice I was covered with mud thrown up by shells bursting near me. I was surprised to get through alive.' On October 25th, he commented, 'It is curious how the war can be carried on. Everyone seems about sick and weary of it, but none the less I think hardly any of us would care for a truce to be patched up that would leave Germany with any power.'

On November 4th, Rev. Allen received the telegram bearing the fateful message that his son had died on November 3rd from wounds. On the following day a letter arrived in which was stated, 'I have had four days at the base, and am just going out again to the line. It is really marvellous how cheerful our fellows keep, especially the infantry, who have the most uncomfortable task.'

His last message was just the official printed postcard, dated November 2nd, on which he had written the words: 'I am quite well.' Second Lieutenant Allen was buried in the Lijssenthoek Military Cemetery at Poperinge, Belgium. In Kenilworth a memorial service was held at Abbey Hill Congregational Church conducted by his father, when appropriate hymns were sung, and the organist, Mr G. W. Bishop, played the Dead March from 'Saul'.

November also brought the news that Lord and Lady Seymour's son, Lt. Commander Arthur Seymour, had been awarded the DSO. At an Urban District Council Meeting the Chairman on behalf of the council congratulated Lord and Lady Seymour on their son's award. He also added that he and his fellow councillors felt that Kenilworth was taking a great part in the war, because several of the inhabitants had gained distinctions, and a large number of men had gone to the front. He believed they were helping as much as any other small town in England. Whilst, however, they congratulated those families whose members had earned distinctions, they sympathised with those who had lost their sons, and in this connection he referred to the death of the son of the Rev. Allen and expressed to Mr and Mrs Allen the council's great sympathy in their bereavement.

Lord Derby's Recruiting Scheme

With the increasing need for more men at the front, Lord Derby, who had recently been made Director General of Recruitment, introduced a new Recruiting Scheme, which consisted of both Recruiting and Tribunal committees. These were set up in Kenilworth in November 1915, with the Recruiting Committee consisting of the members of the Urban District Council, five clergymen, five members of the Working Men's Club, five members of the Conservative Club and nine representatives of the town. The Tribunal Committee consisted of three members of the council and two outside members.

Cards for 516 men who were eligible to join up had been received from the Parliamentary Recruiting Committee and a start was made immediately to interview each man. Within the first five days 277 men had been canvassed and 118 of these had expressed their willingness to join up; the rest were either unfit or had declined service. So many men presented themselves for medical examination to Dr Day that he had to bring in Drs Tweedy and Growse to help. Amongst the applicants for medical examination were two men over forty who were very insistent to be examined and sworn in, but their ages absolutely prevented them being accepted.

There was also some doubt in the minds of married men as to their liability to be called upon for service but the canvassers' instructions on this point were very definite; married men would not be called upon until the single men had been taken. The Prime Minister announced on November 2nd that he had every reason to hope it would not be necessary to call up married men and Lord Derby on November 19th stated that married men would not be called up until young unmarried men had been, and that if these young men did not come forward voluntarily, the married men would be released from

the pledge, or a Bill would be introduced in
Parliament to compel young men to serve. By
the end of November, the Kenilworth Recruiting
Campaign was nearing its completion with a
last minute rush of recruits.

Before the end of the year, news arrived of
the death of Rifleman **George Mitchener**, the
youngest son of Mr and Mrs T. Mitchener of
Warwick Road. He was 19 years old, a member
of the King's Royal Rifles and died of wounds
received in action on the 12th December. Prior
to the war he worked at Dunlop in Coventry.
His two older brothers were also serving their *Rifleman George Mitchener*
country—Harry in the Navy and Albert in the
Army.

Two prominent Kenilworth residents died at Christmas. On
Christmas Day, *The Kenilworth Advertiser* reported the death of Mr
Henry Whateley, the well-known orchid grower of Priory Lane. He
was 58 years old and left a widow and six children. The years to come
were to be a time of struggle for Mrs Whateley as she attempted to
maintain the business on her own.

On Christmas Eve, Lady Seymour passed away at The Firs. Her
loss was mourned at a memorial service at St Nicholas' Church on
December 27th, and her funeral took place at Arrow Parish Church in
Warwickshire.

Meanwhile, unbeknown to the people of Kenilworth at the time,
the close of the year saw the death of another of their number, **Francis
Plant,** a Chief Petty Officer on HMS Natal, who perished on the 30th
of December when his ship blew up in Cromerty Harbour just off
Invergordon in Scotland. At 52, he is the oldest of the men listed on
the Kenilworth War Memorial.

The loss of HMS Natal was a major disaster. She was an armoured
cruiser with a compliment of 704 officers and men, lying at anchor
in harbour over Christmas. Nearly half the crew were enjoying shore
leave, and eight civilians had come on board to celebrate the festive
season at the invitation of Captain Black. Without warning, a fire
broke out in the stern of the ship and almost immediately she was torn
asunder by the explosion of her aft magazines. Almost everyone on

board, including her Captain, was killed. In all, 405 people perished. The official enquiry concluded that the cause of the disaster was faulty ammunition.

Spirits must have been low in Kenilworth at the end of 1915 with still no sign of the end of the war and a further eighteen men from the town having died. The new armies, Kitchener's Mob, the Anzacs (the Australian and New Zealand Army Corps) and the Canadians had all been brought into the fight, but it had been a year of stalemate, mismanagement and muddle, with only partial victories.

Some Kenilworth folk had earlier felt a gloomy foreboding of events to come. A group of people standing on the railway bridge near the Cherry Orchard Brick Works on a late November evening had observed the moon seem to weep in sadness. Drops of fire were falling slowly down the sky like tears of blood. The onlookers were greatly perturbed by this celestial mystery and saw it as a forecast of even more bloodshed. In reality it was a shower of meteorites, which appear annually in the November sky.

Chapter 4

1916 – Horror

On New Year's Day in the morning, the Kenilworth Volunteer Corps assembled at their headquarters, the King's Arms Hotel, to make a presentation to Lance-Corporal **Leonard Henry Reeve** to honour his award of the DCM. The public collection to make a presentation had not been fully successful, but around fifty of the men banded together to pay for an inscribed 18-carat gold demi-hunter pocket watch. It was presented on behalf of the Corps, together with a cheque for £2 6s 6d, by Commandant Kevitt Rotherham. *The Kenilworth Advertiser* reported:

> *Lance-Corporal Reeve was soldierly in the manner of his reception. He advanced smartly to within two paces of the Commandant, and stood at attention. His reply in thanks was brief. 'Gentlemen', he said, 'I sincerely thank you one and all.' The company then gave him three rousing cheers and afterwards marched off to the church service.*

Introduction of Conscription

The British government realised that the voluntary registration under Lord Derby's Scheme had failed to provide sufficient new recruits and introduced the first of a series of Military Service Acts which set out call-up regulations. The first Act called for compulsory enlistment of unmarried men between the ages of 18 and 41, although it also allowed for applications to be made for exemption from the call-up on grounds of occupation, hardship, faith or moral belief.

A system of Military Service Tribunals was set up to assess each application and either turn it down or grant an exemption certificate.

TILL THE BOYS COME HOME

Over seas there came a pleading, " Help a nation in distress! "
And we gave our glorious laddies : honour bade us do no less ;
For no gallant son of Britain to a foreign yoke shall bend,
And no Englishman is silent to the sacred call of friend.

Military Tribunals begin in Kenilworth

The Military Tribunal committee in Kenilworth sat for the first time in February 1916, when there were eight claims for exemption from military service. Five of these were from conscientious objectors, four of them being Christadelphians. They were granted exemption from combatant duties, but were still liable for non-combatant service. The fifth conscientious objector was a bank manager who was granted exemption on double grounds of religious belief and his indispensability to the business he was engaged in.

The three other claims from a licensed victualler, a thatcher's labourer, and a young man in the boot-making business were made on the grounds of domestic responsibilities and indispensability to business. All three were disallowed.

The end of January and beginning of February 1916 saw Kenilworth folk becoming increasingly concerned about the possibility of Zeppelin raids. On three occasions intimations were received that 'the enemy was about' and people wanted to know the best method of letting others know and whether any warning at all should be given.

Police regulations at the time were that no warnings by church bell, siren or hooter were to be given of the approach of aircraft. Instead, members of the local Voluntary Training Corps were to make visits to all houses in the town and request the inhabitants to thoroughly darken them and stay inside

The Town Council discussed at length various alternatives for informing people of the possibility of air raids, including gaslights being dipped three times, but eventually it was decided to continue with the existing house-to-house arrangements.

The first anniversary of the opening of the Kenilworth Red Cross Hospital took place on February 20th. Since that date a year previously, 192 patients had stayed at the hospital. Nearly all of these had been discharged cured and after a ten days' furlough had reported back to their depots. Local people had been particularly generous to the hospital since its opening. When £200 was sought to provide a recreation room this was raised within a fortnight.

The nearby caretaker's house, Stanley House, had recently been taken over to allow for the growing need for more accommodation both for stores and bedrooms for the nursing sisters. Furniture had

The Recreation Room at the Red Cross Hospital

been asked for and within three days everything needed was to hand. The 'Pound Day' had continued every Saturday throughout the year and gifts had flowed in regularly; so much that not a single egg had needed to be bought since the hospital opened.

News from the Front

News of men's deaths at the front sometimes took months to be confirmed and it was not until March 1916 that the official report from the War Office arrived to say that Private **Fred Bayliss**, aged 24, who had been reported missing on 25th April 1915, was declared dead. Before the war he had lived with his uncle, Mr William Bayliss in Mill End. He had volunteered immediately on the outbreak of the war and went to France with the 1st Warwicks six weeks later.

Although during February and March 1916 no Kenilworth men were reported as killed, many of them were having to endure heavy trench bombardment. Private **Harry Bidmead**, of the 1st Lancashire Fusiliers, wrote home to his sister telling her:

> *I suppose you have an account of the terrible bombardment they gave us. I thought our battalion was wiped out absolutely. They blew our trenches to atoms. The earth was just like a volcano for about an hour. I was in the stretcher-bearer's dug-out, so I gave the lads a hand with*

the wounded. It was simply 'Hell'. The shells were dropping right into the trench where we were dressing the wounded. One of the stretcher-bearers had his left elbow shattered, so we were shorthanded. We had two officers wounded. One had a terrible wound in the head and is not expected to recover. I saw some terrible sights, but was so busy with the wounded that they did not take much effect, though at ordinary times I expect they would have bowled one over. Our artillery sent over 7,000 shells during the bombardment, and there was nothing but large craters where their trenches had been, so they did not get off scot free.

Sid Parrock (who was to survive the war) wrote home to say that he thought the war would be over by August as the Germans were getting short of ammunition and tired of war. He felt the health and spirits of the chaps were excellent, with everybody chummy and anxious to help one another in every possible way and in spite of the bombardments the men lived very well in the trenches. They had bacon for breakfast, roast beef for dinner, bread, butter and jam for tea, and generally two issues of rum per night, so he felt he couldn't grumble.

The Blizzard

In England the weather was playing havoc. On the night of Monday, 27th March, driving hail and snow accompanied by a strong wind brought chaos to Kenilworth and many other parts of the country. The storm caused heavy damage to telephone and telegraph wires, causing unsuspecting car drivers on Tuesday morning to become entangled in the wires. Damage to property was slight, the worst misfortune happening to the Abbey Hotel. Half a row of twenty tall trees bordering the bowling green at the hotel were blown down in a mass across Priory Road taking with them the fencing and wall for a stretch of thirty to forty yards. There was no case of personal injury although about a hundred or so lambs were lost in the neighbourhood. Hundreds of trees, however, were destroyed and every road without exception was blocked. The Coventry Road was soon reopened but the Leamington and Warwick roads remained blocked for two days and minor roads were impassible for even longer.

On the Stoneleigh Estate the fallen trees ran into thousands. There was a whole stretch of about 200 trees levelled in Crackley Wood, and Mr Percy Martin's screen of fir trees at his residence, The Spring, was

Kenilworth after snow

sadly depleted. Narrow escapes from injury were many. A tree fell across the wash-house at Beehive Cottage, Birmingham Road and one on to the roof of the typewriting office in Priory Road. In common with the rest of the country, the local train service was absolutely disorganised, and the mail train arrived five hours late. *The Kenilworth Advertiser* reported, 'some bold spirits had pushed through the gale at 5.30 on Tuesday morning to catch their usual train, but these early birds had to go with the sluggards four hours later.'

The War Effort continues

Lincoln Chandler's family, like so many families within the town, were busy participating in activities for the war effort, both at the front and at home. Their eldest son, Alfred, who had been on divisional headquarters staff since March 1915, had recently transferred, at his own request, to a Royal Field Artillery battery in the fighting line and soon afterwards was mentioned in General Douglas Haig's dispatches for distinguished service. Mr Lincoln Chandler himself had taken over as Platoon Commander of Kenilworth Volunteer Training Corps 'C' Company from Mr Bates, whilst his wife had started a collection for a 'Kenilworth' bed at the Royal Star and Garter Home at Richmond Hill, London, a hospital for helplessly wounded and incurable soldiers. The aim was to raise enough money by the end of August so that a bed could be nominated for a Kenilworth soldier should it be needed. On several occasions the family provided entertainment for the soldiers both at the hospital and at their home, Abbotsfield. Daughter Marjorie did her bit by singing songs at concerts to raise money for the local Red Cross Society.

Mr and Mrs Cay, who lived at Woodside and were equally involved in the war effort, received the news in early May that their only son, 36-year old, Lieutenant **Albert Jaffray Cay**, had been declared missing after the battle of Katia in Palestine on Easter Sunday, 23rd April.

Disaster in Palestine

The national newspapers published an account of the incident at Katia in which two squadrons of the Worcester Yeomanry were attacked by a combined German, Austrian and Turkish force five times their strength, with four mountain guns. The subsequent fighting involved a further Worcester squadron, two squadrons of the Warwickshire Yeomanry and the Gloucester Hussars. Fighting alongside Lieutenant Cay were his 33-year old brother-in-law, Captain Leslie Cheape, a famous polo player, and his 22-year old cousin, Second Lieutenant Sir John Henry Jaffray, the 3rd Baronet. All three officers were reported as missing. However, the Turks claimed that they had captured 23 prisoners, and so there was every reason to believe that they might be unharmed prisoners of war.

No further news of Lieutenant Cay, his brother-in-law or cousin was heard until July 1916 when they were reported as having been killed in the action on 23rd April. The following is a correspondent's account of the Yeomanry fight in the Sinai Peninsula on that day:

> On April 22nd, 1916, two squadrons of the Worcestershire Yeomanry were ordered to Oghratina, a post five or six miles in front of Katia, to protect a detachment of Royal Engineers, who were digging wells, and doing other work there. They were connected with Katia by telephone. The third squadron of the Worcesters and two of the Warwickshire Yeomanry took part in a small expedition against a Turkish camp some eight or ten miles off. One squadron of the Gloucestershire Yeomanry took the place of the Worcesters at Katia.
>
> On the morning of the 23rd there was a dense fog. Oghratina telephoned Katia about 4.30 a.m. that they had been attacked, but the

enemy had drawn off. They were reattacked later, and at 7 a.m. the wire was cut. Very heavy firing was heard till 7.15 at Oghratina, then all was quiet. There was no doubt that the garrison were surrounded in the fog, heavily fired on, and finally rushed by far superior numbers. The two squadrons must have put up a great fight, as the loss of eight officers killed and three wounded out of thirteen officers shows. The numbers of men killed and wounded must be large, but it is not yet known. Many of the prisoners writing home seem to have been wounded.

The Katia garrison of the Gloucesters, which was heavily attacked about 9.30 a.m., was reinforced by the third squadron of the Worcesters. Two squadrons of the Warwicks operated on the right flank (these three squadrons had, earlier in the morning, destroyed a Turkish camp), and two squadrons of the Gloucesters on the left flank. They made a great effort to defeat the Turks, but the Katia force was overcome.

Officers of the Worcestershire Yeomanry. 1914.

Back Row:—Lieut. M. C. Albright, Lieut. H. N. S. Wilson, Lieut. G. R. Wiggin.
Third Row:—Lieut. J. Blakeway, Lieut. N. M. Pearson, Lieut. L. G. Haynes, Lieut. R. E. Colville. Lieut. A. Hickman, Lieut. R. J. Watts, Lieut. Sir J. H. Jaffray, Bart., Capt. N. H. C. Russell.
Second Row:—Chaplain, Rev. Canon A. C. Deane, Lieut. W. B. Chamberlain, Lieut. E. S. Ward, Lieut. E. Holland, Lieut. A. J. Cay, Capt. F. S. Williams-Thomas, Capt. Lord Hampton, Capt. O. Teichmann, R.A.M.C.
Front Row:—Capt. H. Tomkinson, Major Hon. J. C. Lyttelton, Major Hon. C. J. Coventry, Lieut.-Col. The Earl of Dudley, Major H. A. Gray-Cheape, Capt. W. H. Wiggin, Capt. and Adj. L. St C. Cheape.

The Worcester squadron leader (whose horses fortunately were not put out of action), with the assistance of his squadron sergeant-major, managed to bring up a lot of his horses, and get off 60 or 70 men, but the remainder of both Gloucesters and Worcesters were either killed or taken prisoners after a gallant fight.

The Warwick and Gloucester squadrons on the flanks managed to draw off from the fight, the latter suffering very severely from four guns which the enemy brought into action. Both regiments were skilfully handled, but were quite out numbered.

As the Warwickshire Yeomanry were involved at Katia it was initially thought the four Kenilworth men with that regiment, Sergeant-Major W. Nixon and Troopers Allen, Crouch and Hubbard, might have been killed. Fortunately all escaped injury. It was Trooper **Arthur James Hubbard** who described the fighting and their escape in a letter to his parents who lived in Stoneleigh Road:

I expect by the time this reaches you, you will have had news that we have been in action again. We had a lively day amongst the confetti just at the time that you at home were singing peace and goodwill to all men (Easter Sunday). I told you in my last letter that we were going thirty miles beyond the canal into the Sinai desert patrolling, and minding some wells in the Katia district. After two days marching we arrived there, and for the first week things were quiet, but last week it began to get lively as we met several enemy patrols, and one of their aeroplanes dropped bombs. Last Saturday night we set out with a squadron of the Worcesters to raid an enemy camp about ten or twelve miles away, and without knowing went right between two enemy forces, and luckily did not run into them, or someone would have got hurt. When we got to their camp we found only six left, whom we took prisoners, and the tents we looted — it was fine sport. We arrived back at our camp at Hamassah at 9.30 on Sunday morning to hear that the Worcesters and Gloucesters camps were captured by the enemy, and so we had to go out again to try to drive them out of the Worcesters' camp at Katia, four miles away, and there we had a rare battle, which lasted until four in the afternoon, when we had to retreat because we were being surrounded. The Worcesters had four big guns against them, but we escaped them, so we didn't have many casualties. About 4 o'clock we began a rear-guard action back to our camp, when our aeroplane brought a message to say another force of the enemy were close to our own camp coming from the opposite direction, so we had to leave in a big hurry, leaving our camp and all our kit just as it stood and get back to Kantarah.

We are now back at Ballak, and think it was only by a miracle that we got out of as tight a corner as it was possible to be in. It was not until we were back here that we found we were up against a strong force of Austro-Germans, as well as Turks, four or five times our number, who had attacked Duidar, between us and the canal, and practically cut us off.

Although Trooper Hubbard escaped injury at Katia, he died the following April from wounds received in action at Gaza. Lieutenant Albert Cay, his brother-in-law and cousin were never found and are remembered on the Jerusalem Memorial in the Jerusalem War Cemetery in Israel. This cemetery, which is set amid olive trees, is at the north end of the Mount of Olives and over looks the city of Jerusalem. The memorial commemorates over 3,000 soldiers of the Egyptian Expeditionary Force from the United Kingdom, Australia, New Zealand and South Africa who fell in Egypt and Palestine during the 1914-18 war and who have no known graves.

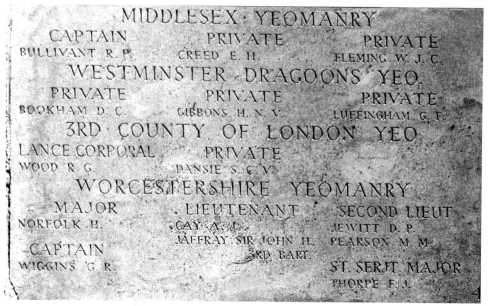

The names of Lieut. Albert Cay and his cousin Sir John Jaffrey on the Jerusalem memorial

Full Conscription introduced

In May 1916, a revised Military Service Act was introduced which brought all men, regardless of marital status, between the ages of 18 and 41 under the provisions of the existing Military Service Act. It also allowed the War Office to extend the service of time-expired men whilst there was a war and to re-examine men rejected as physically unfit.

Shortly before conscription began, the death occurred in France of Lance-Corporal **Harold Charles Martin**. He was 25 years old, with the 14th Battalion Gloucestershire Regiment, and had worked for the Kenilworth Post Office before the war. He was killed by a sniper on the 2nd May

For King & Country.

and is buried in Merville Community Cemetery, Nord, France. The town of Merville at that time was a billeting and hospital centre and practically all of the British burials in its cemetery were those of men who died in these hospitals.

Kenilworth military tribunals continued to be held and that month two interesting cases demonstrated how certain occupations carried an exemption from taking up military duties. Market gardening was a certified occupation but nursery work does not appear to have been, as is shown in the following cases reported in the local newspaper:

> *Alfred Douglas, married, a nurseryman of Whitemoor, applied for a second time for exemption. His father appeared for him, and stated that applicant was in sole charge of the nurseries at Whitemoor and that one of his sons had joined the Navy. The application was refused.*
>
> *Joseph Clifford, School Lane, Kenilworth, market gardener, in the employ of Mr Croydon being in a certified occupation was granted total exemption.*

Harry Hincks Butcher's shop in Warwick Road

Not all men in exempted occupations applied to remain at home. Kenilworth butcher, **Harry Hincks,** who had two shops in Warwick Road, put up a notice to say that his business would be closed from 17th June 1916. Refusing to ask for an exemption, he had attested under Lord Derby's scheme and when his group was called up he took up service straight away.

The *Kenilworth Advertiser* saw this as the 'true British spirit', throwing up a very prosperous trade and placing himself entirely at his country's service. They wished him good luck and a safe and speedy return.

Life goes on in Kenilworth

By the end of May, the Kenilworth woods were 'wearing their spring blue carpet of wild hyacinth', a wonderful sight that encouraged crowds of people on their annual pilgrimage to Crackley Woods where hundreds of children picked armfuls of bluebells.

Empire Day was celebrated at the local schools. At St Nicholas' school the flag was hoisted, and as the children marched into school they saluted it. The Headmaster, Mr Hacking, addressed the whole school on 'Empire Day and its meaning' and endeavoured to inculcate into the children a true love for their country, a sense of their duty towards it, and of true and false patriotism. Later in the day a concert took place with the children singing many patriotic songs. A very extensive list of ex-scholars who were serving their country was read out, followed by Annie Walker reciting the poem, 'How Sleep The Brave'. The children then stood while the roll of honoured dead was read, which already totalled ten former pupils. After more choruses and recitations and a song by Madge Carter, attired as 'Britannia' with trident, shield, and flag, the whole school sang 'Land of Hope and Glory' and finally the National Anthem at the end of the day.

Two events caused great excitement in Kenilworth in May. First an aeroplane ran out of petrol and was forced to land in Mr Bostock's clover field, just beyond the cemetery. A crowd gathered quickly and gave the police a busy time keeping them out of mischief. However, after obtaining 12 gallons of petrol, the aeroplane was able to take off again.

The second event was the arrival of the London Film Company at the castle. They used the ruins as a setting for many scenes in a cinema film entitled 'When Knights Were Bold'. The townspeople were presented with the rather incongruous sight of some 135 warriors in armour, chain mail, tin hats and breastplates arriving at the castle by motor-car. The castle grounds were full of ladies in gorgeous creations, fat old monks, beauteous and virtuous nuns, a heroine in rags, a bold bad knight who wanted to kidnap the leading lady and actor Mr James Walsh as the rescuing hero. There were 28 scenes and episodes concerned with Kenilworth Castle and 100 scenes in all.

Some of the scenes were set in Warwick Castle, but the bulk were taken in the company's studios. A local flavour was added to the film as a horse belonging to Kenilworth coal merchants, Messrs. Stickley, took a prominent part in this film. He served as a 'charger' for a gallant knight, whose weight he bore with as little concern as when he pulled his daily load of coal.

More Tribunal Cases

Many of the Military Tribunal cases during the summer months of 1916 were from farmers who were finding it increasingly difficult to keep with up with the necessary work on their farms. The Royal Agricultural Society had recently issued a statement to the effect that it had been agreed between the War Office and the Board of Agriculture that farmers should be allowed to retain one able-bodied man to every team of horses, and one such man respectively to every 20 milking cows, every 50 store cattle and every 200 sheep. Nevertheless, local farmers were still having to appear before the tribunals to plead on behalf of their workers.

Fred Snelson, who farmed 200 acres at Chase Farm, applied for total exemption for his son, aged 19, and his cowman Edward Davison. He explained how difficult it was to get labourers at this time, his cottage having been empty for nine months. Conditional exemption was granted to each of these men until January 1917.

Likewise, local farmer, Mr Gee, made application for conditional exemption for his cowman, John Sawyer. Mr Gee had tried female labour, but said it was impossible to replace men. This case was also given a conditional exemption until January 1917.

One local resident who was having to apply continually throughout the year for exemption for her workers was Mrs Whateley who, since the death of her husband, ran the nurseries and orchid houses. In July 1916 she applied on behalf of her orchid house foreman, James Newton, aged 40 and married with four children, who had been passed fit for general service. Mrs Whateley already had two sons at the front and the remaining one was about to be called up. She explained that Mr Newton was the only one of her employees who understood orchids and his departure would involve her in great financial loss. Conditional exemption was granted to Mr Newton to December 1st 1916.

Loss of Lord Kitchener and a local lad

At the beginning of June 1916, everyone in Kenilworth shared the tragic news of the death of Lord Kitchener, the Secretary of State for War. Lord Kitchener had been on his way to Russia to boost Russian morale and help keep them in the war. On the 5th June his ship the HMS *Hampshire* struck a mine off the Orkneys and sank. For a long time the British public refused to believe that Kitchener was dead. He represented England in a way no other wartime leader had done. For one Kenilworth family the loss of the *Hampshire* was a very personal blow for on that ship was Able Seaman **Harry Mitchener**, the second son of Mr and Mrs Mitchener, of Warwick Road. They had already lost one son, George, who had been in the army and a third son, Albert, was out in the trenches at this time.

KENILWORTH SAILOR ON
KITCHENER'S SHIP.

NO NEWS OF HARRY MITCHENER

ABLE SEAMAN MITCHENER.

Able Seaman Harry Mitchener was 26 years old and had been in the Navy ever since he was a boy of 16. At the time of the commencement of the war he was serving on the *Hampshire* on the China station, the boat taking part in the pursuit of the German commerce-raider *Emden* and subsequently conveying the prisoners from that ship to Malta. He was making good progress as a sailor, had recently passed an examination to become a Leading Torpedo Seaman and was looking forward to promotion and a successful naval career.

Lord Kitchener was remembered at church services throughout the town and a memorial service for Harry Mitchener was held at St John's church.

The Battle of the Somme

Within a few weeks of Lord Kitchener's death, his Volunteer Army of two and a half million men or 'Kitchener's Mob' as they were commonly known were to take part in their first major offensive against the Germans on the Western Front, on the plain of the Somme river. The first day of the Battle of the Somme was the blackest day in the history of the British Army. At 7.30 a.m., on the 1st July 1916, a continuous line of British soldiers went 'over the top' and began to walk slowly towards the German lines. Many of them believed that the enemy positions had already been destroyed in the previous week's long artillery bombardment, but the Germans had scarcely been affected by this and emerged from their deep shelters to mow down the British soldiers. By the end of the day the British had suffered 60,000 casualties.

The Battle of the Somme was to continue relentlessly until November 1916, with the line only moving forward approximately five miles, at a cost of a million casualties, including 420,000 British. Twenty-two men from Kenilworth lost their lives in the Battle of the Somme .

Private **George Henry Swann** of Cross Row, was the first to be killed. He was with the 10th Worcestershire Regiment, and was reported missing on the 3rd July and later said to have been killed, although his body was never found. He is commemorated on the massive Thiepval Memorial alongside thousands of others who were similarly lost.

Sapper Jim Smith

Ten days later, Sapper **Herbert James Smith** (known as Jim) from Mill End was killed in action in Trones Wood. He was only 18 when war broke out but decided to answer the call to arms, leaving his apprenticeship at Messrs. Alfred Herbert, the toolmaking firm in Coventry, to join the signal company of the Royal Engineers.

He had been in France for a year and was said to be a lad of always cheerful disposition, never complaining of any of the hardships he must have experienced and always doing his utmost to prevent his parents feeling more anxiety about him than could be helped. In his most recent letters home he tried to reassure his parents by writing, 'Don't worry; I'm all right.' He had sung in the choir of St Nicholas' Parish Church for eleven years and on his last leave home at the end of December 1915 had taken his accustomed place amongst them.

The details of Jim's death were sent to his parents by a comrade in his section, Niel Williams, from Leamington. He wrote:

At 1 a.m. yesterday we were ordered to move forward to ------ which had been taken and lost several times during the last few days, our brigade having been commanded to capture it at all costs before dawn. It was the duty of our signal section to keep up communication with the forward troops making the attack. We arrived at the point from which operations were to commence at about 2.15 a.m. having come through a very heavy bombardment without a casualty.

I was sent back to the brigade, and at 6 a.m. the sad news came through of the very brave manner in which Jim met his death. They were ordered to get into communication with the battalion assaulting the wood, and Jimmie immediately led two other men over with the wire. A shell burst just as they were about to enter the wood, and poor Jimmie was killed instantaneously, the other two men being wounded. … Although he was the youngest member of the section, Jimmie was always regarded as one of the pluckiest, and it will be difficult to replace him. He was a favourite with all the boys … everyone of whom looked on him as a brother.

Many of the men were killed at the Somme as they courageously tried to help others. **William Drane-Overs**, the sergeant-drummer who had gone to France to form a band, was acting as a stretcher-bearer when he fell victim to a shell explosion. Similarly, **Walter Barber**, of New Row, a private with the Royal Warwickshire Regiment, was killed by a shell whilst helping to carry wounded men out of the firing line.

Seniority in rank did not guarantee a soldier's life. Major **Guy Egerton Kidd**, DSO, was killed by shell fire on the 26th September. He had lived at Ladbrook House, New Street, Kenilworth for a few years up to the outbreak of the war and had been at the front since March 1915, first as adjutant of the 4th South-Midland (Howitzer) Brigade, Royal Field Artillery and since October as commander of a battery.

Private Walter Barber

Captain **Trevor Carlyon Tweedy**, the 21-year old son of Dr Tweedy, Kenilworth's general practitioner, was killed in action at High Wood on the 15th September. He had first gone to France in 1915 and had been invalided home with trench jaundice after six months, but after recovering rejoined his battalion, the Northumberland Fusiliers, in France, in March 1916.

Dr Tweedy at this point in the war had been appointed the senior medical officer at the Second Birmingham Hospital. It was from this hospital that men were sent to the Red Cross Hospital at Kenilworth which had now been extended to take up to 40 casualties. Reporting on the condition of these men who had returned from the Battle of the Somme, *The Kenilworth Advertiser* stated that they had very slight wounds and took this as confirmation of the daily press reports which said that the majority of the cases from the Somme were only slightly wounded. It was believed that because of the big preparatory bombardment there was practically only machine gun and rifle fire for the men to encounter and the bullets usually made very clean wounds. What the press failed to understand and convey to the general public was that the injuries were slight because the majority of the men had been killed outright.

An active member of Kenilworth's Red Cross Society was killed in action at Bazentin-le-Petit on the 11th August. Second-Lieutenant **Norman Ward**, 21, from Barrow Road, had only been in France for a month when he lost his life. He was with the 11th Battalion Royal Warwickshire Regiment, and previous to the war had worked for his father's currier's firm in Kenilworth. He was also honorary secretary of the St Nicholas' Sunday Schools. After his death the vicar, writing in the parish magazine recalled that it had only been a few weeks since he came to make his Communion before starting for the front. After the service he found his way to the vestry and said 'Goodbye Vicar, I'm off to the front at last. The "big push" is on, you know.' Scarcely three weeks had passed when the news came that he had been killed in the attack. He was moving his men to a safer position when he was struck down.

Throughout the summer months of 1916, it was still thought that this 'big push' would reach a triumphant conclusion and Sir Douglas Haig, Commander-in-Chief, requested that there be no slackening of output of munitions even for a moment. He appealed to the patriotism of the workers of the country and the Government decided that in the national interest there should be no August holiday either general or local. The Kenilworth Tannery was now asked for a double output of tanned leather and was employing 100 men and 12 girls to fulfill the order. Although there was no official holiday in August, a spell of hot weather in the middle of the month led to an unprecedented run of attendance at the Kenilworth swimming bath with 800 bathers in one week.

With the thousands of men involved in the Battle of the Somme it was inevitable that brothers would be fighting together and getting killed together. This happened to several Kenilworth brothers. Just six months after receiving congratulations from the Chairman of Kenilworth Council and the presentation of a gold watch in recognition of his DCM, Corporal **Leonard Henry Reeve** was killed by gas poisoning on the 17th July. He was 24 years old. The sister-in-charge of the clearing station, wrote of the regrettable manner of his death in a letter to his parents:

He was admitted to this hospital on the 14th July suffering from gas poisoning. The Germans had fired some gas shells into the trenches, and our men did not know they were gas shells and had not got their helmets on. We did all we could to relieve him, but we could not prevail. He was not in a condition to speak. I got your address out of his log-book. He passed away at 2 p.m. today 17th July. He will be buried in the military cemetery attached to this camp by the side of so many of his fellow soldiers who have laid down their lives for their country in a righteous cause.

A memorial service was held at St John's church on the 12th August in tribute to Corporal Reeve. A few days later came the news that his older brother, Alfred, had also been killed in action. Private **Alfred Reeve**, 32, of the Royal Warwickshire Regiment, left a widow and six children. They lived at Fairview Place, Kenilworth. He was killed on the 25th July by a fragment of a shell striking him in the back.

Family Losses

Two brothers were killed three weeks apart, but the sad news arrived in Kenilworth on successive days. Lance Corporal **Edward Whateley**, with the 8th South Staffordshire Regiment, was reported missing after an attack made by his regiment on July 10th. The news was sent to his wife in a letter from a Kenilworth man in the same regiment, Company Quarter-sergeant George Bricknell, who had since learned that Edward 'had been killed bravely doing his duty facing the foe' and that his body was found and buried by another division.

The following day his brother's wife received a letter to say that her husband, Tom, had also been killed in action. **Thomas Whateley** was a Rifleman with the King's Royal Rifles and was killed by a shell at Albert on 1st August 1916. The two brothers were sons of Mrs Whateley, a widow, of Castle Green; they do not appear to be related to the Whateley family who ran the nurseries in Priory Road.

Edward Whately

Often brothers fought together in the same battalion. Private **Edgar Thompson**, 22, had his twin brother serving alongside him in the 18th Battalion, King's Royal Rifles Corps. When Edgar was killed in action on the 18th September, his twin faced the horrendous task of having to send home to their parents the sad news of his brother's death. The twins, who came from Priory Road, had both volunteered in October 1915 and were only in France a few weeks.

Similarly, Private **William Hickman**, aged 27, and his brother Harry, aged 26, from Mill End, were both serving with the Berkshire Regiment. They were together at the front for almost three weeks in August 1916 when Harry was seriously wounded in the thigh and foot. William carried his injured brother back through the fighting lines to safety. Harry was taken to hospital while William returned to the front to continue fighting. A week later William was reported missing. His body was never found and he was numbered amongst those killed. Harry endured several operations to deal with his injuries, but lived to survive the war.

The other Kenilworth men who lost their lives at the Somme in 1916 were Second Lieutenant **Charles Sydney Reed** who had worked in the laboratory of Sir Oliver Lodge at Birmingham University before

enlisting in the spring of 1915, Corporal **Henry Victor Gardner** of Spring Lane who was killed by a sniper, Corporal **Alfred 'Punch' Skelsey** aged 43, who had enlisted in the army 23 years previously and served throughout the South African war, **William Chaloner** a sergeant with the King's Shropshire Light Infantry and Private **Frederick Howlett Pittaway**, of St John's Terrace, a volunteer with the Royal Warwickshire Regiment.

Corporal **Charles Austin Butler** and Private **William Henry Watson** were the first two Catholic men from Kenilworth to be killed. Special masses were held for them in succeeding weeks at St. Augustine's church and the school flag was flown at half mast.

Thomas and Mrs Whately

Wilfred George Daniells, a 19-year old private with the Royal Marine Light Infantry, who had volunteered at the outbreak of the war and had served at the Dardanelles, was killed on the 13th November. Second-Lieutenant **George Lushington Colomb**, DCM, although originally with the Royal Fusiliers, had entered the Royal Flying Corps after gaining a commission and was killed when his plane crashed on November 22nd in France.

Military Medal for George Bricknell

In spite of this long catalogue of deaths throughout the summer and autumn months of 1916, many Kenilworth men did survive the Battle of the Somme, including **George Bricknell** who was promoted to Company Quartermaster-Sergeant and awarded the Military Medal for gallantry on the field. The Military Medal was a new award which had been instituted by Royal Warrant just four months earlier in April 1916. The medal was of silver and awarded to non-commissioned officers and men for individual or associated acts of bravery at the recommendation of a Commander-in-Chief in the field.

George Bricknell was honoured for his bravery when two companies, including his own, were almost surrounded by the enemy; he took a message to the commanding officer for reinforcements, returning through a torrent of shot and shell with the commanding officer's reply. In late September 1916 he was further promoted to Sergeant-Major. The Kenilworth Working Men's Club took up the idea of a suitable public recognition being made to him for the honour he had gained. Two hundred and fifty circulars were printed asking for subscriptions to a testimonial fund. It was proposed to make the presentation to him at a public meeting at the first opportunity.

Military Tribunals continue

With the heavy loss of men at the front over the summer months it was imperative to replace them as quickly as possible and by autumn 1916 the Military Tribunals were working hard examining all those who had applied for exemption from military service. It was not just the farmers and owners of commercial premises who were having to appeal for exemption for their workers. Well-to-do people in Kenilworth were now having to appeal on behalf of their staff.

In June, Miss Dora Schintz, of Thickthorn, applied for the exemption of her estate steward and a stableman. The steward was given military exemption on condition he undertook work in a munitions factory, which he agreed to do. The stableman was given conditional exemption but later in the year this was withdrawn because of new orders from the War Office with regard to men employed in stud stables. As he was only an assistant stableman he would now have to undertake military duties, although it was agreed to give him 14 days notice before he was called up.

Mr Albert Cay of Woodside applied for the exemption of his chauffeur, a married man with two children. The claim was made on the ground of national interest in that Mr Cay was the sole proprietor of a Birmingham firm which, in addition to making certain articles now required by the Government, supplied lenses for use in railway lamps. Owing to ill-health Mr Cay had been advised not to travel by rail and therefore needed a chauffeur to drive him to and from Birmingham. The car was also needed by Mrs Cay for her to carry on her various charitable works. Mr Cay had tried to find a substitute for the chauffeur but had been unable to find anyone suitable. The tribunal granted exemption until January 1st 1917, to give Mr Cay time to find a substitute.

Some local residents did not believe in applying for exemption for their employees. Mr Lincoln Chandler had refused to apply on behalf of his gardener, Albert Waterton, who was liable for military service and this caused a nasty situation to arise. Mr Waterton, who lived at Abbotsfield Cottages in High Street, had started to make himself objectionable in various ways, so much so that Mr Chandler was obliged to appear before the Kenilworth Divisional Sessions in September 1916 to have his former gardener ejected from the tied cottage.

As summer ended and the winter nights drew in, St John's Church decided to abandon their Sunday evening services and hold afternoon services instead. This was to comply with the lighting restrictions which would have resulted in a large expenditure in effectively darkening all the church windows.

The wounded soldiers at the Red Cross Hospital, who were only allowed out of the hospital for two hours in the morning and two in the afternoon, welcomed diversions in the long winter evenings.

One of these was a visit by 14 members of the Ordnance Choir from the Coventry Ordnance Works who gave the men a very welcome evening of entertainment, including choruses of 'Comrades in Arms' and 'Drake's Drum'.

Military Cross for Arthur Chandler

There were two promotions for the Chandler family in November. Eldest son, Alfred, although only 25, was promoted to Major and awarded the Military Cross. The citation for his award stated that:

> *During operations this officer has commanded his battery with conspicuous ability. On many occasions he ranged his battery from very exposed positions to ensure the accuracy of his barrages. He has several times been mentioned in dispatches for good work.*

His father, Lincoln Chandler, was also promoted, being made Commander of 'C' Company of the Kenilworth Volunteers with the rank of captain.

Meanwhile Mrs Chandler had completed her fund-raising for the bed at the Star and Garter Hospital. Kenilworth people had been very generous including one young lady, a Miss Bishop, who had given all her earnings as a motor-van driver to this and similar charities. A cheque for £1,045 had been forwarded to their headquarters, a contribution which would allow preferential consideration to any Kenilworth man wishing to be admitted to the hospital.

Mrs Whateley appeared again before the Military Tribunal in December on behalf of her worker, James Newton. She stated that the orchid houses were now being run by Mr Newton with the help of only a woman and a boy, since four men had left and joined the forces. Lord Ernest Seymour, a member of the Tribunal committee, felt that orchids were an unnecessary luxury in times of war, but Mrs Whateley countered that thousands of pounds had been spent in forming the collection and such a sum should not be thrown away. After a heated debate in which Lord Seymour suggested that in war times the dust heap was the best place for orchids and Mrs Whateley responded that if the Government would compensate her, it would be a different matter, the tribunal finally granted a further three months' extension.

Despite the grim news received from the front during the last few months, preparations for Christmas began in earnest all over the town and many clubs and organisations sent Christmas parcels to Kenilworth soldiers and prisoners of war. The Tannery Company sent each of the 60 men who had joined the forces, a parcel of tobacco, value 5s, whilst the Caledonian Corks Lodge of Oddfellows held a concert to raise funds so that each of their soldier members would receive a present. St John's Church sent a Christmas card to everyone serving in his Majesty's forces from the parish. This numbered nearly 200 men.

A survivor of the Battle of the Somme was home on leave for ten days just before Christmas and the local newspaper was keen to hear about his experiences. Twenty-year old Corporal **Fred Wilkshire** who was with the King's Royal Rifles had seen action in several battles before the Somme. *The Kenilworth Advertiser* reported that:

> *Having been at the Somme from July 3 till he came home it does not require much imagination to realise that the young man has had a rough time. He is however one of the bright cheery Tommies of whom one reads, and his experiences have not changed him, for he is typical of the Tommy of popular fancy. …. He had nothing to report, he informed our representative, but a little judicious questioning as to who took Guillemont brought him out. His battalion had as big a hand as any. He has seen the 'tanks' at work and has been thankful for their company. He recalls a certain sunken road at Guillemont which,*

A British tank in action

when the artillery had ceased firing on it, and when the 'tanks' had stopped crawling into it and out of it, belched forth a hurricane of machine-gun fire. He says the infantry had little to worry them when they rushed for the road – but quite a lot of grave-digging. The worst position which they were called upon to take that day was the quarry, which caused quite a deal of trouble before they were surrounded and gathered in – some alive and some not. The prisoners on that very day well exceeded a thousand.

The tanks that he spoke about had been introduced as a new special weapon of war in September 1916. The secrecy which surrounded them led the troops to refer to them as the 'Hush! Hush! Brigade'. A young man from Kenilworth had been selected to work as a gunner on these tanks, much to the surprise of the local newspaper. Corporal **Dudley White**, son of Mr and Mrs Frederick White of Castle Rest, Castle Road had enlisted in 1915 at the age of 18 and was described as a bright, yet frail-looking, pale-faced boy who had worked at the mill and later at Eykyn's motor garage. It was felt he hardly looked the stuff of which good soldiers are made, yet he came out trumps being made a lance-corporal within two weeks of enlistment, and then was picked for the important task of working on the new tanks. In a surprise attack on the Germans, he was inside one of these tanks for 14 hours and was later reported as 'playing Jonah in this land whale, and lumbering across "no man's land" to scatter destruction and death to the enemy. This time the "Tank", after carrying out useful work, took fire, although they had to make a bolt to shelter under machine gun fire. Corporal White got a bullet through his cap, touching his ear.' Dudley White, like Fred Wilkshire, was to survive the Battle of the Somme, but both these brave Kenilworth lads were to lose their lives in the following year.

By the end of 1916, the war had become a continuing saga of relentless horror and death. Possibly to spare the feelings of the general public— or to conceal the extent of the slaughter—the accounts of the war in the newspapers began to be censored. The reporting of men's deaths became much briefer, and fewer soldiers' letters were published. Prominence was shifted to focus on local news.

Chapter 5

1917 – Unremitting Death

T he report of a railway accident just outside Kenilworth took precedence over war news in *The Kenilworth Advertiser* during the last week of January 1917. The 9.25 p.m. passenger train from Coventry to Kenilworth ran into the back of a stationary goods train. The goods train was badly damaged, particularly the guard's van, but fortunately the guard was not in the van at the time. A loaded coal wagon was pitched down the embankment and the contents of the guard's van and several mineral wagons littered the sides of the track. The passenger train was also badly damaged but both driver and fireman were uninjured and the passenger coaches remained on the track. Most of the passengers' injuries were relatively slight, mainly bruising. The site of the crash was near the signal-box midway between Kenilworth and Coventry and some passengers attempted to walk in the dark to Kenilworth, but were stopped by railway officials. After a long wait, an engine was sent from Coventry to take the coaches and passengers back via Berkswell to reach Kenilworth at about 1 a.m. The line was cleared for the early morning trains.

Kenilworth Station

Kenilworth War Allotments Committee

Towards the end of 1916, the British government became very concerned about the provision of food for everyone at home. A new Defence of the Realm Regulation empowered the Board of Agriculture to take and use vacant land for food cultivation and local authorities were delegated to carry out this measure to increase home-grown food supplies. Councils were given the right to take land and grow crops upon it as long as those crops only took up to a year to grow.

The Kenilworth Council passed a resolution that a War Allotments Committee be formed and by January 1917 this was in full operation with members considering various sites around the town that could be used. There were 126 applications for allotments from the townsfolk. Sites offered included a field in School Lane owned by Lord Clarendon, land in Whitemoor Road belonging to Mrs Whateley, a field in the centre of Abbey Fields, a small portion of land in Barrow Road belonging to Councillor Randall, land behind the Cherry Orchard brickyard belonging to Mr Hawke's executors and land in Bertie Road belonging to Sir Michael Lakin. Mr Cay had generously offered three acres of land at Windy Arbour rent-free for the duration of the war. Twenty-four allotments were required in the St John's area of the town and Miss Schintz was approached about the land she owned there. She readily agreed to lend some and also offered to have it laid out into allotments.

Applicants would be allocated land as near their homes as possible and the suggested rent was 10s per fifth of an acre plot. The Allotments Committee proposed to purchase seed potatoes to sell at cost to the allotment holders. The Kenilworth Surveyor, Mr Sholto Douglas, was also given authority to grant permission to applicants to keep pigs provided that they complied with the conditions recently published by the Board of Agriculture and the Local Government Board.

With still no end to the war in sight and the urgent need for yet more men at the front, the British government informed the military tribunals that all men who could be spared without serious detriment to work of essential national importance, or who had no other very strong grounds for exemption, should be made available for military service as soon as possible, at the latest by March 31st, in order that they could be put under training.

Mrs Whateley, of Priory Nurseries, appeared again before the Tribunal in early February, only this time she applied for exemption of her youngest son. She stated that her business was a precarious one, and it was essential that this son should be retained, as both older brothers had already joined the colours. This was her fourth application and the military opposed it on the ground that it was unnecessary for a single young man to be so employed, particularly when Mrs Whateley had five or six men in total working for her. The new government order made compliance with the application a practical impossibility, and it was not granted. The military agreed, however, not to call up Mrs Whateley's son without 14 days' notice.

New regulations for the volunteer force came into effect in February 1917. Men were now required to pass a medical examination and sign a pledge declaring they would serve in the force for the duration of the war and keep themselves efficient by attending the prescribed number of drills during that period. Of the 42 Kenilworth men medically examined that month, 40 passed the necessary tests satisfactorily.

Death of a Kenilworth Nurse

The name of only one woman is inscribed upon Kenilworth War Memorial amongst those who died in the First World War. This is Constance Emily Mary Seymour, the youngest daughter of Lord and Lady Seymour, and a probationer nurse with the Queen Alexandra's Imperial Military Nursing Service. She died at the Connaught Hospital, Aldershot, on Monday, 12th February 1917, aged 29.

Constance, like her mother, took part in much charitable work in Kenilworth. Before the outbreak of the war she was honorary secretary of the Kenilworth Voluntary Aid Detachment of the British Red Cross Society and helped with the organisation of a Welfare Centre for mothers and babies. She was anxious to become a trained nurse and went to the Warneford Hospital, Leamington for voluntary training. When the Kenilworth Red Cross Hospital was opened at the Parochial Hall, Constance became one of its nurses and afterwards joined the staff of the Cambridge Military Hospital at Aldershot. She returned from there to help nurse her mother before Lady Seymour's death and then resumed her work as a nurse at the Connaught Military Hospital in mid-summer 1916.

In November she contracted a bad attack of measles from a patient, and was incapacitated for several weeks. Upon her return to duty she contracted a cerebro-spinal fever, and died within two days. Her funeral took place at Aldershot with full military honours. Eight senior officers of the RAMC acted as bearers, while the band of the corps headed the cortege from the hospital to the cemetery. All the nurses who could be spared and members of the RAMC followed the gun-carriage on which the coffin was carried, and a firing party of the corps attended. After the body had been committed to the ground three volleys were fired over the open grave, followed by the 'Last Post'.

Her death was seen as just as significant as that of any fighting soldier. Her obituary in the *Kenilworth St Augustine's Church Magazine* spoke of the military funeral with firing party and band being an honour which implied:

> *... a soldier's life, a soldier's work, a soldier's risks ... Her duties in the hospital wards have exacted a life that was young, full of promise, and unselfish unto death. She fell a victim to duty – carried off by one of those insidious diseases that are as rapidly fatal as the bullet on the battlefield. She died a martyr of charity in the endeavour to rescue and save the lives of the sick and wounded soldiers, a work demanding heroism and self sacrifice .....*

The Allotments

Within a month of land being secured it had all been plotted out ready for digging once the frost had gone. Forty large plots and sixty-four small had been let and Mr Douglas had secured four tons each of King Edward (main crop) and Eclipse (early) seed potatoes, which would be sufficient to set about twelve acres of land. On the 20th February a very well-attended meeting was held at the Council Schools to hear a talk by Mr Dunkin, FRHS, the County Council expert, who gave a detailed lecture upon the best methods to produce the crops most needed: potatoes, peas, beans, carrots, parsnips, beet and different varieties of the cabbage family. He urged the gardeners to get the land broken up at once and recommended farmyard manure and soot and the need for frequent hoeing in summer time. He asked them all to work with a will, remembering the hardships of the long lines of heroes in France. He said that financiers and munition workers were sending their message, and let it not be said of them at home that they had failed to deliver the goods.

Over the next few weeks most allotment holders put in strenuous work on their gardens with about half choosing to have their land ploughed. Councillor Randall offered the use of one of his horses to assist in this ploughing when the weather permitted. The surveyor had also been instructed to have notice boards erected upon each allotment field, on which to display the Government Order making trespass on allotment land an offence under the Defence of the Realm Act.

Difficulties for Tradesmen and Farmers

By the spring of 1917 Kenilworth tradesmen and farmers were finding it increasingly difficult to run their businesses with so many of their employees having enlisted. Mr Dowell, a local baker, applied for temporary exemption for John Twigger, aged 18, who had been passed for general service. Appearing before the military tribunal, Mr Dowell stated that he was already so short-handed in his bakery that should Twigger be called up he did not see how he could get through his work. He said that the young man was in the bakehouse from 5.15 a.m. to 12.30 p.m. and delivered bread in the afternoon. Mr George, a member

Women and Children helping Mrs Edwards on The Elms Farm in Coventry Road

of the tribunal, expressed the opinion that the system of delivery of bread was wasteful of labour. In Coventry, he said, a system of pooling had been adopted, and only the biggest bakeries were now making bread. The application was refused.

Likewise Mr Smith a farmer from Pleasaunce Farm appeared before the tribunal to appeal for his waggoner, **Norman Parkyn**, aged 18. Mr Smith stated that he had 366 acres of land, 113 of which was arable. He had planted 25 more acres of wheat than usual, and he urged the necessity of the lad remaining until the spring planting and summer cultivation had been finished. The military opposed on the ground that Mr Smith already had more labour than other farmers, and that young healthy men were urgently required for the army. The application was refused, but the military undertook not to call him up until June 1st.

Norman Parkyn's fate was sealed by this military tribunal. He was called up later on in 1917, went to France, and was taken a prisoner of war in March 1918. He remained a prisoner until after the war had ended, not being released until January 1919. This was followed by a spell in hospital in Scotland until July that year, but his health was broken and he died at home on the 13th August 1920. Norman's elder brother, **Jacob Parkyn**, another employee on Mr Smith's farm prior to the war, was also to lose his life in 1917 when he was killed in action in France on 27th August.

A case that aroused considerable discussion at a military tribunal in March was that of Colin Stewart, 33, single, motor-driver for Mr Dudley Docker. The man had been passed as fit for labour abroad and the military opposed his exemption, feeling he could easily be replaced. The application for exemption was made on the grounds of national interest as Mr Docker was employed entirely on Government work, and the retention of his driver was essential to him. However, it was elicited that Mr Stewart was not entirely employed in driving Mr Docker, and that on account of his medical history a serious effort to obtain a substitute had not been made. The application was refused, but the military agreed not to call him up until May 1st.

Mrs Whateley once more applied for the conditional exemption of the manager of her orchid house Mr James Newton. The military would only grant temporary exemption until September, conditional on him being engaged eight hours per day on the work of food production in other parts of the nursery. Mrs Whateley agreed to these terms.

On the Western Front the German army had drawn back to a stronger position known as the Hindenburg line. There seemed no end in sight, but a new plan was put in action for the French and British to break the German line south-east of Arras and in April the British pushed forward in the Battle of Arras. The same month the United States finally agreed to declare war on Germany. Two million American men volunteered and three million were drafted.

Supporting the cause

The Red Cross Hospital was being kept continually busy with patients. In April 1917, there were 32 patients, with 15 more due to arrive shortly, which would be a record and fill all the available accommodation. Additional quilts were needed for the beds for these expected new patients and the Ladies' Working Party from St John's Church, with the help of friends, held an 'all day' working party and was able to complete 30 quilts.

Easter Monday on the Western Front was notable as the day the Canadians seized Arras Ridge and advanced over three miles in one morning. Back at home it proved to be a cold, bleak, snowy day and prevented the usual day trippers visiting Kenilworth. The weather must have improved as the following weekend the members of the Kenilworth Voluntary Training Corps were called into action with the task of lending a helping hand to the wives of men on service who had no one to cultivate their gardens or allotments.

The Kenilworth Advertiser described this activity as if the men were going into battle:

Red Cross Hospital Patients playing Cricket in Abbey Fields

The Kenilworth Volunteer Corps on parade for Inspection, May 1917

Captain Chandler, Lieutenant Corser and Sergeant-major Beck, led fully forty members of the corps to the attack on Sunday afternoon, each shouldering a spade. Kenilworth people are familiar with the personnel of the local men, etc. nine out of ten quite unused to hard manual labour, and many of them getting on in life. It speaks volumes for their training when the extent of ground dug in the 2$^1/_2$ hours of last Sunday afternoon is seen. They worked right heartily, and maintained the pace right through, digging over half-an-acre of land, and planting quite a deal of it too.

Their hard work was really appreciated by the serving soldiers. Captain Chandler received a letter later in the year from Rifleman Drane:

I write to thank you and the N.C.O.'s and men of your company for so kindly digging and planting my garden. It is good and kind to think that you are all trying to do what you can for us out here. I know they must have had a rough job on, for I have been out here nearly three years, and it has only had a little done to it during that time. My wife tells me they have done it first-rate.

He continued his letter by saying:

I get the local papers, so I can follow the doings of dear old Kenilworth closely. I am sorry to see some more of our Kenilworth men have paid the great sacrifice during the last offensive. I am afraid there is harder fighting in front of us all yet, as I consider this war is only about half-way through. The sooner people realise that this war is serious to all countries concerned, and take a conscientious view of things in general, the sooner it will be over. I know everybody wants to get it over; then the best way is to put the shoulder to the wheel and help with all their might and main.

Most weeks now the local paper reported a further death of a Kenilworth man, including that of **Fred Wilkshire** who had survived the Battle of the Somme. On returning to France from his leave at home over Christmas he had been promoted to sergeant and then was killed in action near Bethune on the 5th April. Fred, who lived in Bridge Street, had worked as a gardener before the war for Mr Quick, the architect, and was a member of the Abbey Hill Football Club. He was the brother of William Wilkshire, who had been killed at Gallipoli in April 1915.

Whilst the majority of the men were killed in action on the battlefield or died from their injuries abroad, many of the injured were sent home to hospitals all over England. Corporal **Alfred Aitken**, from White's Row, and also a member of the Abbey Hill Football Club, died on the 26th April 1917 following the amputation of a leg at the Bristol Southern Hospital. He had been in hospital for four months and had already undergone six operations in attempts to save his leg. He was with the Oxford and Bucks Light Infantry having enlisted in early 1915, and had been wounded in France. The story of how he came to

Sergeant Fred Wilkshire   *Corporal Alfred Aitken*   *Private Edgar Vincent*

be wounded is itself a brave one. Another corporal was feeling unwell, so Alfred took his place in the firing line and a sniper's bullet wounded him in the leg.

White's Row was also the home of Private **Edgar Arthur Vincent** who died shortly after Alfred Aitken. He had been injured in the Battle of the Somme in July of the previous year and had returned to France in January, after spending Christmas at home following his discharge from hospital. His family were first told that he had been severely wounded whilst in action on the 10th May 1917. Not hearing any further news, his father wrote to his company officer to enquire about him. He replied to say that Edgar had been severely wounded in the head on that day and was removed from the trenches by a stretcher party, but was alive when last seen, although it was not known to which hospital he had been taken. It was the end of June before his parents had the official news that Edgar had died of his wounds. He was 20 years old and had worked at the Triumph Works in Coventry before being called up.

Harry Hincks

Nearly a year after the local butcher, Private **Harry Hincks**, had shut his business and gone to the front, news of his death came to the town. He had been killed instantaneously by a shell in the trenches on the 8th May. His death was deeply felt by the townsfolk.

The Kenilworth Advertiser, whilst acknowledging that every case of a brave man's death called forth sympathy, felt that in the case of Harry Hincks there were circumstances which gave the event an unusual sadness. He never needed to go to war. He was 39 years old, almost out of military age, and engaged in an essential branch of food supply, conducting two butcher's shops under conditions of labour shortage. He could readily have obtained exemption from military service had he cared to apply to the Tribunal, but he had for a long time expressed his intention of taking his share in the war.

When his group was called up in June 1916, he had immediately closed down his business and joined the county regiment. He was not sent abroad immediately but spent several months in training. One of his instructors in the first month was local man, 21-year old Second-

Lieutenant **Norman Ward**, from Barrow Road, who was later killed at the Somme.

After training, Harry was transferred to the Duke of Cornwall's Light Infantry and went to France in October 1916. He was then transferred to the Machine Gun Section in March 1917 and saw continuous service until he met his death. He had lived and worked in Kenilworth for fifteen years and was a remarkably popular man with a wide circle of friends. He left a widow, a daughter of 12 years old and a baby boy of three months whom he had never seen.

Matters of Food

By the spring of 1917 all the allotment holders had finished planting their crops and the potatoes were starting to come up. The subject of providing enough food for everyone in England was at the forefront at this time and the need to cut back on the amount of food eaten was also of great concern. A local Food Economy Campaign Committee was set up under the chairmanship of Dr Growse and a public meeting was held at the Abbey Hotel Hall when Mr E. J. Carter, H. M. Inspector of schools, spoke of the necessity for cutting down on bread because of the difficulty of getting corn into the country. Literature was distributed giving particulars of economical cookery and a further meeting was held in the Drill Hall when Miss Bolton, another H. M. Inspector, and others spoke and gave cookery demonstrations.

Even on Empire Day, the 24th May, the need for economy and frugality was stressed. A thousand Kenilworth schoolchildren assembled in the Abbey Fields and after lustily singing the National Anthem and giving three cheers to His Majesty, the Town Crier, Sergeant R. Barwell, brought the assembly to order with his bell and his cry of 'Oyez! Oyez! Oyez!'

Chairman of the council, Mr Randall, then read the King's Proclamation exhorting and charging the people of Britain to practice the greatest economy and frugality in the use of every species of grain, to reduce the pre-war consumption of bread by at least one-fourth, and to refrain from using flour for pastry, etc. In addressing the children he said that in addition to celebrating Empire Day they had a further duty before them, which was to pledge themselves to economise greatly the consumption of bread.

He explained that the soldiers sent from the colonies had naturally left their countries depleted of men to grow grain: that there was a shortage of ships to bring the grain; and that grain-laden ships were being sunk by submarines; and he asked them to eat as little bread as possible, and on no account to take any away from the table.

All were asked, to sign a pledge to abide by the King's Proclamation, and to wear a purple ribbon as a sign of their patriotic intention. He also asked the children to refrain from buying sweets, for sugar was very scarce. 'Save your pennies,' he said, 'and put them in war savings, and so help your country.' By following these lines he concluded they would be helping to defeat the enemy, whose object was to smash our Empire.

National Herb Growing Association

As well as food being in short supply there was also a dearth of medicinal herbs which had formerly come from Germany. These were now being grown again in England, something which had practically ceased prior to the war, and wild herbs were also being used. A committee for Kenilworth district, calling itself the Kenilworth and District Group of the National Herb Growing Association was formed, to undertake the collection and drying of these herbs, with the Hon. Agnes Leigh as president.

It was decided that each district should specialise in just a few medicinal herbs, and the Kenilworth association devoted its attention to growing opium poppies and marigolds and gathering foxglove leaves. The poppy heads were used for the extraction of opium which was required in large quantities to ease the suffering of wounded soldiers. The flower petals of the marigolds provided an invaluable ingredient for ointment, whilst foxglove leaves were picked about mid-June, when the plant was in flower, and digitalis (a heart stimulant) was extracted. The association planned to obtain a dryer, which would be installed in the Gate House at the castle.

Whitsun Holiday

As Whitsun 1917 approached, news from France was of further advances by the British. For many people at home their thoughts turned towards the holiday, and Kenilworth was crowded with thousands of holiday-makers on Whit Monday. Trains were crowded, and hundreds more walked from Coventry.

Kenilworth Station

Most of the day trippers had the foresight to bring their own food, although some had to return home hungry because all the bakers and tea shops were cleared of their stock early in the day. This was not the only trouble. The railway officials soon recognised that the service of trains would be utterly inadequate to cope with the traffic returning in the evening and ceased to issue tickets at two o'clock. Only people booking before that hour, or who had bought return tickets, could get back to Coventry by rail.

The bus service was running at full capacity and could not materially help the situation, and many a tired tripper found that another five miles walk awaited him at the end of the day. *The Kenilworth Advertiser* reported that:

> *Never had such scenes been witnessed at the railway station. For the 7.10 train there was a crowd of people on the platform which more than filled every single foot of space in the train, and left others to swell the crowd already waiting (with doors closed) in the large area in front of the booking office for the 8.25 train. Anyone arriving at that time was refused admittance; even Birmingham people had to make the best of it, and either go to Coventry by road and there catch a train for home, or find sleeping accommodation in the town.*

The month of June 1917 brought several changes both nationally and locally. Due to the huge increase in anti-German feeling throughout Britain, the royal family decided to change their family name from Saxe-Coburg-Gotha to Windsor. Locally a new vicar, the Rev. Joseph William Dennis, arrived at St Nicholas' Church and the Kenilworth Castle estate was sold.

The estate had been divided into 57 lots, including 14 farms, smallholdings, 108 acres of woodlands and also properties in Kenilworth, and they all came up for auction at the Craven Arms Hotel, High Street, Coventry on the 27th June. Two of the farms, Castle Farm and Grounds Farm, were bought by Mr Gee junior, the tenant, for £7,000 and £6,300 respectively.

The Belgian refugees who had been staying at Bridge House for over two years moved to Montfort Cottage in High Street as their numbers had diminished and a smaller house was now sufficient. Negotiations then started for Bridge House to revert back to a ladies' school, for which purpose it had previously been used.

By July the war allotments were looking good. Turf had been late being broken up, but with the copious rains and hearty digging the crops were looking nearly as good as those on long worked soils. The Arthur Street allotments were particularly pleasing and a heavy crop of potatoes was expected.

Death of Kenilworth's former GP

Dr Reginald Carlyon Tweedy, the town's former general practitioner, became a victim of the war when his health broke down under the strain of his work and he died at Newquay on 12th July 1917 at the age of 48. Dr Tweedy had been in practice for 23 years in Kenilworth and was also medical officer to the Warwick Union for Kenilworth and the large surrounding district. When war broke out he spent his holidays in 1915 and 1916 as an operating surgeon in France. He finally relinquished his private practice in Kenilworth in August 1916 and, accepting the temporary rank of major in the R.A.M.C., took up the duties of senior resident surgical officer of the 2nd Birmingham War Hospital.

He was married with four children and suffered a terrible blow in September 1916 when his eldest son, Captain Trevor Carlyon Tweedy, was killed. Dr Tweedy's funeral took place at Kenwyn in Cornwall, his family's home, with his brother, the Rev. Harold Carlyon Tweedy officiating.

Simultaneously a memorial service was held at St Nicholas' church. The church was filled and *The Kenilworth Advertiser* felt it was probable that on no such an occasion had so many people assembled in Kenilworth, which reflected the esteem and affection in which Major Tweedy was held by the people of the town.

With the war now almost into its third year, Kenilworth residents were reminded to keep sending letters to the men at the front. One unusual reminder came in the form of a poem written by Gunner E. J. Vaughan, of St John's, Kenilworth. He was with the Royal Field Artillery and wrote the verses whilst in hospital in Malta and they were published in *The Kenilworth Advertiser*:

TOMMY'S MAIL

What a prize is Tommy's mail?
Whether on desert, hill, or vale,
His thoughts by day, his dreams by night,
Centre around the 'Blighty' mail.

The hospital patient brightens up,
He does not look so pale
As the word goes through the ward,
'Here comes the English mail!'

The black sheep of the company,
Kicking his heels in gaol,
Feels just a bit ashamed
When from home he gets his mail.

The youngsters rush from their sport,
Old soldiers leave their ale!
What miracle, indeed, is this?
Why– the bugle sounding 'Mail!'

Fathers, mothers, sisters, brothers,
Wives, sweethearts, do not fail;
Write him something all the time,
Let Tommy have his 'mail.'

Passchendaele

Letters and news from home were always important, and would have been particularly so at this time as things were 'hotting up' at the front. The British Commander-in-chief, General Haig, was planning an offensive with the intention of capturing the Passchendaele-Broodseinde Ridge, and continuing with a movement designed to reach the Belgian ports which were occupied by the Germans. 'Third Ypres'—the official name of this battle—lasted from the 31st July until 6th November 1917, but is commonly known as the Battle of Passchendaele – a battle where the deterioration of the weather in the final part of the campaign gave it an evil reputation for horrors in the mud. It resulted in 400,000 British and Empire casualties.

Twelve men from Kenilworth were killed at Passchendaele. Six of these were with the local Royal Warwickshire Regiment and included Regimental Sergeant-Major **Joseph Pratt,** with the 10th Battalion, who died on the 20th September at Ypres from wounds received in action. Sergeant-Major Pratt was 41 years of age, a long-service man, well-known in Kenilworth, where he and his parents lived for many years at Washbrook House, and later in New Street. He had married Miss Bayliss, of Clifton Terrace, a teacher at St Nicholas' Schools. *The Kenilworth Advertiser* described him as 'an extraordinarily fine specimen of manhood, 6ft 2in in height, and splendidly proportioned.'

Sergeant **Bert Charles Bannard** was the first Kenilworth man to die at Passchendaele being killed in action on the 13th August near Ypres. He was 27, lived in Albion Street, and was with the 1st/7th Royal Warwickshire Regiment having joined up in September 1914. He had been promoted to lance-corporal in early 1916 and then sergeant in September 1916. His brother (both parents being dead) had received a letter from his captain, confirming the sad news, and stating that Bert was an ideal non-commissioned officer and would be much missed by his officers and men. Apparently his last words as he fell were, 'Carry on, men – I'm done.' Before the war Bert was employed at the Daimler Works, Coventry, as a polisher, but was also the trainer of the Abbey Hill football team. The whole football team had enlisted and Sergeant Bannard was the fourth member to lose his life.

Private **Ernest Alfred Frazer**, nicknamed 'Chuffy', was killed by a sniper on the 27th August near Ypres. Before the war he worked at

Kenilworth Tannery and served with the Territorials, being mobilized and sent immediately to France in August 1914 when war was declared. There he served for three years, being with the 1st/7th Royal Warwickshire Regiment when he was killed at the age of 21. He was the son of Mr H. Frazer of 13 Albion Street, Kenilworth, and had two brothers also serving—George with the Gloucesters in France, and William with the Royal Warwickshire Regiment in Mesopotamia.

His company sergeant major wrote to Mr Frazer on September 1st saying that Ernest had been his orderly for 18 months, and he felt he must write:

> *We were attacking on August 27th, and were held up by rifle and machine-gun fire when 'Chuffy' got hit in the shoulder by a sniper. He could not tell me where he was hit, as he could not feel anything. He only lived for three minutes. He was a brave lad, feared nothing, and was always ready and willing to do anything.*

A further letter arrived in Kenilworth in September 1917 with reference to Ernest. A fellow soldier, Private A. Tebby of Spring Lane, wrote to Mr Randall at the Tannery mentioning that he had seen a lot of Kenilworth boys in France, and described how the meeting with familiar faces brightened him up. Upon hearing that Ernest had been shot he said, 'I managed to scramble over hedges and ditches, and when I got there they were just burying Ernest Frazer.'

Private **James Pressley Tookey,** also with the 1st/7th Warwickshire Regiment, died on the 4th October aged 36. He was the husband of Jessie Mansell Mary Tookey of 26 Spring Lane and left three children.

| *Sergeant Bert Bannard* | *Private Ernest Frazer* | *Private James Tookey* |

Before the war he worked at Messrs. Courtaulds at Coventry. His chum, Private Arthur Skelcher of Coventry, sent the sad news to Mrs Tookey that her husband had been killed instanteously during an enemy attack. James had gone to the rescue of a wounded officer when a bursting shell killed them both. Several months later Mrs Tookey was to receive a letter from the sister of the captain to whom her husband had been orderly, showing how, after a period of devoted service to his captain, Private Tookey sacrificed his own life in attending to a mortally wounded officer. She wrote,

> *It seems that Captain Croall was leading his company into action on October 4th, when he was shot through the head by a machine gun bullet. He was conscious for a few minutes, and asked Private Tookey to bring the sergeant-major. Your husband tried to get him, but owing to circumstances could not do so. He returned to my brother and started to bind up his head, when he was shot and killed instantly. This is all the news we have received, and we are very anxious to know where my brother is buried. If you have received any news about Private Tookey we would be so glad if you would let us know, for as he was killed at the same time as my brother, they would probably be buried near together. My brother was home on leave in September, and he was telling us that he had the best man in the battalion for his orderly, Private Tookey was always so good to him, and looked after all his kit so well. We shall always feel grateful to your husband for his kindness to my brother. The other officers told us that his devotion to my brother was remarkable, and I cannot tell you how much we appreciate it.*

The bodies of Private Tookey and Captain Croall were never found; they are commemorated on the Tyne Cot Memorial.

The other two men with the Royal Warwickshire Regiment were Private **(William) Jacob Parkyn**, 22, of The Pleasaunce, Kenilworth, with the 6th Battalion, who was killed by a shell on

Private William Jacob Parkyn

27th August and Corporal **John Welch Bradshaw,** of the 1st/7th battalion, who was killed by a sniper on the 4th October. He was 32 and lived at Ingleside, Warwick Road and had joined up in 1914 with the Leamington 'Pals' Company.

Sometimes men who were related were killed within weeks of each other. This happened to **Ernest Letts** and **Reginald Jack Collett** who were brothers-in-law. Ernest was killed in the Battle of Passchendaele whilst Jack was killed at Cambrai. Private Ernest Letts, of 65 Henry Street, was with the Gloucestershire Regiment. Before joining up he had been a gardener at Hillcrest, Kenilworth, was 31 years old and married but had no children. He had joined up in May 1916,

Private Ernest Letts and his wife Ada, sister of Jack Collett

and was in France with his regiment, in the following autumn. He was invalided home after Christmas 1916 with trench feet, which kept him in hospital for six months. He spent a leave at home in August

Private (Reginald) Jack Collett

1917 before returning to the front and was reported killed in action at Ypres on the 9th October 1917.

Ernest's wife had seven brothers, four of whom were also serving in France and in his last letter to her he mentioned that he had run across her brother Ernest. It was another brother, Private Jack Collett, who was killed the month after Ernest Letts. Jack, who had worked in Kenilworth Post Office prior to joining up, was with the Royal Fusiliers and was reported seriously wounded and missing on the 24th November 1917. Nothing further was heard of him and he was declared 'killed in action' on that day. He was 24 years old and is commemorated on the Cambrai

Memorial in France, whilst Ernest Letts is buried in the Poelcapelle British Cemetery in Belgium.

Sergeant-major **George Bricknell** MM, was home on leave during August 1917 and at a crowded gathering at the Working Men's Club was presented with a demi-hunter 18-carat gold watch, subscribed to by over 200 Kenilworth people, in recognition of his gallantry. He returned to the front shortly afterwards, but by November his wife and friends were becoming increasingly concerned as no news had been heard from him for three weeks. They then heard he had been wounded, but no other news. Enquiries were made which proved fruitless

Sergeant-Major George Bricknell MM

and it was not until February 1918 that definite news was received that he had been killed by a large shell explosion at close quarters on 12th October 1917.

Other local men to die at Passchendaele were Private **Carlton Rivers**, 25, of Freza, Waverley Road, who had been a very promising art student prior to the war and was with the Machine Gun Corps. He was killed on the 22nd August. Bombardier **Arthur Albert Sadler** of the 15th (Warwick) Brigade of the Royal Horse Artillery was killed in action on the 30th August. He was a married man from St John's Avenue and before joining up had been the manager of the Bear Inn. **John Garrett**, from Spring Lane, a Gunner with the Royal Field Artillery, was killed in action at Poperinghe on the 5th September. He was married and had two small children.

Dudley Nevill White, the gunner working on the tanks, was killed in action by a shell which struck his tank, while the machine was in operation at Poelcapelle on the 9th October. The lieutenant in charge of the 'Tank' sent the following letter to Dudley's father:

Dear Mr White,—I am very sorry to have to inform you that your son Dudley, the finest and bravest boy I have ever met, was killed in action on the 9th of this month. He was in my own crew, and we went into action at dawn on that morning against some strong points at Poelcapelle. From the start we were shelled heavily, and about 8.30 a shell struck the 'Tank', killing your son who was at his gun – he was a gunner – instantly. His death must have been painless, for he never uttered a word, being hit along the back and right side. The Corps has lost a brave soldier and my Company a dear comrade with his death and you have our utmost sympathy at this sad blow. Any of his effects he may have left in his kit will be sent to you. He is buried beside the 'Tank' in Poelcapelle, and a braver boy never rests under the Belgian soil. I send the sympathy of the whole Company to you and your family

Yours sincerely J. A. Cogner, Lieut.   Gunner Dudley White

A month after Gunner White's death a different tactic was introduced at Cambrai, when a mass use of tanks was employed for the first time. Significant ground was taken by using tanks but later in the month a German counter-attack retook all that had been gained earlier. The war was proving unrelenting.

Autumn Activities

In Kenilworth, the Tannery was extremely busy. During the past year the firm had supplied sufficient leather for over a million pairs of boots with leather being despatched for boots for the Russian, Italian, Serbian, Belgian and Greek armies. This enormous output had meant adding extensions at the works and also using the very latest appliances and means for tanning leather. At this time the Tannery was the largest employer of labour in the town.

The approach of autumn in Kenilworth had resulted in a very heavy crop of blackberries and ever-mindful of the need to provide food, the Board of Education and the Food Production Department came up with a scheme for organising the collection of these blackberries by schoolchildren to be made into jam for the troops. Half-holidays were granted to the children to go blackberrying and it was hoped to carry on the scheme on each Friday during the month of September. The children brought the berries to stores which were established at the schools. They were weighed and paid for at the rate of 1d per pound. After two weeks the schoolchildren of Kenilworth and the neighbouring villages had picked and sent off 2,173 lbs of blackberries, and further half days of picking were planned.

War Heroes Recognition Fund

By November 1917 there were 692 men from Kenilworth serving in the army or navy, which was over 10% of the town's population. Kenilworth Urban District Council resolved to arrange for a public recognition to those Kenilworth men who by acts of gallantry had won special marks of distinction. A committee was appointed and it was hoped to raise £300 out of which presents would be made to those men whose special services had already received recognition. In the event this fund was very slow to attract support, probably because of the incessant calls upon the public for funds at this time. By December when the roll of honour had risen to 715, with 66 having lost their lives, the War Decoration Recognition Fund had only reached £75. *The Kenilworth Advertiser* felt that censorship of news from the front was the cause of this shortfall. It stated:

> *If only the public could be made to realise what a man undergoes in the trenches in the ordinary course of warfare, and then to conceive what the super-heroes face to deserve mention, there should be no difficulty in the matter at all – but in these days of censorship we at home and in comfort do not in the slightest understand or grasp what war is.*

At the end of November there were fewer men than normal at home on leave, but one soldier who did manage it was **Private James Harris,** of the South Staffs Regiment, the former Kenilworth postman, who was spending a few days in Kenilworth with his family. Up to this point he had been on active service for most of the war with the exception of a short spell when he was wounded in the early days.

Food Economy

The supply of food was an increasing problem by the end of the 1917 and it was also becoming difficult to obtain a sufficient supply of milk as pasture land was now coming under the plough. The Food Control Committee formulated a tentative scheme under which milk supplies would be ensured for infants, invalids and nursing mothers. Flour for bread-making was also difficult to obtain and bakers were having to resort to adding a quantity of potatoes to the bread mix.

Just before Christmas the Kenilworth Council held a special meeting to consider opening a communal kitchen in the town. This was a further aim at economy by cooking in bulk to help those people with longer working hours who were hard-pressed to find time for cooking. The kitchen would be self-supporting, with those benefitting paying the cost of their meals. The Food Control Committee asked the Council for two ground-floor rooms and the loft over them in the cottage adjoining the council office. They asked for this to be provided rent-free with the Council paying for any kitchen equipment which would not be covered by any grant they might receive from the Food Controller. The Council granted the Food Control Committee's application.

News of men's deaths in the months before Christmas must have added to the gloom of a town already mourning so many of its men who had given their lives this year. On the afternoon of the 10th November Mr and Mrs R. H. Clive, of Fieldgate Lawn, Kenilworth, received a telegram telling them that their elder son, Flight Sub-Lieut. **Reginald Dennis Clive**, R.N., had met with a serious accident whilst flying in Scotland. They travelled to Edinburgh to the hospital where he had been taken but arrived too late to see their son alive. He had sacrificed his life by swerving his aeroplane to avoid some boys when making a forced landing because of engine trouble. Dennis Clive was only 19 years old and had joined the Naval Air Service whilst still a student at Caius College, Cambridge, nine months previously. He is buried in St Nicholas' churchyard.

In early December news arrived of two Kenilworth soldiers, one killed in action and the other missing. Private **Bert Gillam** of the East Surrey Regiment was killed in Belgium on December 1st. He was 28 years old, married with one child, and lived at Mill End. He had been a gardener at Wilton House but had left there for Courtaulds in Coventry. He had joined the army eighteen months previously and been in France for a year. He is buried in Bleuet Farm Cemetery, Elverdinghe, Belgium. Bleuet Farm was a dressing station in 1917 and the cemetery was constructed in a corner of the farm.

Private **Harry Reynolds** was reported missing on the 3rd December. He was a baker employed by Mr F. Fancott and enlisted in September 1914 in the Army Service Corps, in which he served three years before being transferred to the Durham Light Infantry. He was married with two children. No further news was received of Harry and he was presumed killed on the day he went missing. He is commemorated on the Cambrai Memorial.

Three days before Christmas the son of a local councillor was killed

in action. Lance-Corporal **Cyril W. Carter** was the youngest son of Mr
C. J. Carter, draper and outfitter, of The Square, Kenilworth. He was 25
years old and had joined the Oxford and Bucks Light Infantry in April
1915, going to Salonica the following autumn. He returned to England
at Christmas 1915 suffering from trench feet which incapacitated
him until the following May. Upon recovering he was sent out to
France, where he served to September 1917, when he spent ten days
leave at home, returning again to his battalion in October. On the
22nd December, whilst in charge of a Lewis gun team during heavy
bombardment near Passchendaele, he was killed instantaneously by a
shell. His regimental chaplain wrote to his parents to say that he was
buried on the Westrobosheke Road, about one mile behind the front
line. The precise location of his burial place is now unknown and he is
commemorated on the Tyne Cot Memorial.

Lance-Corporal Carter had been educated at Mr Taylor's college in
Kenilworth, alongside two other Kenilworth soldiers killed in action,
Norman Ward and Dudley White. The following spring their parents,
together with those of Dennis Clive, gave a new baptistry in the south
aisle of St Nicholas' church as a memorial to the four young men.

The year 1917 had been one when the Allies had been confident of a
decisive breakthrough, yet in spite of great improvements in artillery,
more aircraft and the introduction of tanks, this had not happened and
had resulted in another year with an enormous numbers of deaths.
Kenilworth lost 33 men and one woman. Due to censorship, people at
home were not always aware of the terrible time the men were having
at the front and life at home was becoming increasingly stressful.

People were having to work incredibly hard, for longer hours, and
were now facing shortages of food and other essential items. Christmas
Day 1917 saw large congregations at both St Nicholas' and St John's
churches, with people evidently feeling a great need to come together
at such a difficult time.

Chapter 6

1918 – Salvation

A National Day of Prayer and Intercession was held throughout Great Britain on Sunday, 6th January 1918, and once again the local churches had large attendances. The King's Proclamation asking his people, 'to pray that we may have the clear-sightedness and strength necessary to the victory of our cause,' was read out together with lists of fallen men. At St John's the Vicar had received a letter from a local soldier:

GOD BLESS DADDY AT THE WAR

Tho' 'tis but a baby's whisper, but I know that God will hear,
Keep on praying, baby darling, there are angels list'ning near;
Far away, and yet so near me, guardian angels hover o'er,
Lifting your wee voice to heaven, " God bless Daddy at the war ! "
Daddy knows, and God is near, "God bless Daddy ! " I can hear,
What those lips are praying for is " God bless Daddy at the war ! "

Just a few lines to thank you and the congregation and parishioners of St John's parish for the Christmas card and greetings which has been sent to me. I wish all of you a very bright and prosperous New Year. While we are out here fighting for victory and peace, I hope and trust that the people at home will attend God's House and pray for us out here because we have got a very anxious time now in front of us. If they will only pray and have faith in God we shall all pull through, and if they will always remember us in their prayers they will be doing their duty at home just as much as we are out here.

Kenilworth people were, of course, praying for the soldiers abroad and constantly thinking about them. The War Heroes Recognition Fund had now nearly reached £80 and a Prisoner of War Fund had been started to send fortnightly parcels of food and necessities to Kenilworth 'boys' who were being held prisoner in Germany. Mr Hetherington, who started the fund, stated, 'These lads have done their level best for us, and are now in durance vile and on the verge of starvation. Just think! Every penny is a mouthful. Let us meet the lads on their return with the knowledge that we did not leave them to be fed on charity. 'Tis cold fare. Our duty is clear.'

Known prisoners in Germany at that time were Private Jack Harris (late of 3 St John's Terrace), Private Ernest Baylis (Mill End), Private F. W. Adkins (Park Road), Corporal E. Dilworth (New Row), and Private F. A. Roser (Henry Street). Private George Sheepy, whilst still a prisoner, had been transferred to Switzerland, and there were at least two Kenilworth men held prisoner in Turkey—Private Floyd and Private E. Faxon—although it had not been possible to communicate with either of them.

A further soldier's letter received in Kenilworth at this time showed that although the men obviously wanted to be back home they were determined to finish the job they had started. Mr and Mrs J. Freeman of New Row, received the following letter from their 23-year-old son Jack, serving with the Royal Engineers in Egypt:

> *I am writing you this just to let you see that I am still alive and kicking 'Somewhere in a wilderness in Palestine.' I expect it seems very strange to you at home to think that your lads are fighting on the very plains on which our Lord lived and worked. It appears funny to me when I come to be by myself and think things over; but this is not the first battle that has been fought in this wilderness, for battles, I am told, were fought here even before Christ came on this earth.*
>
> *Little did I think that I should be amongst these sun-burnt, tanned-faced, and blistered soldiers, to march across this sacred land. We find it most monotonous work waiting, watching, and toiling day after day in this awful heat, but I am proud to think I am amongst these men. If you only knew half of what we are doing I'm sure you would be most proud of us. Of course, as you know, I am forbidden to say much . . . . I shall be glad to get back to my dear old home country, but I want to see this job through, then I can return home knowing that I have done my share of it.*

Sapper Jack Freeman was one of the lucky ones and arrived back safely at the end of the war.

Not so lucky were three Kenilworth men who died in January and February. **James Marvin** of Bulkington Cottages, a married man with

one child, was killed in action on the 6th January.
He had joined the Dublin Fusiliers in the autumn
of 1914 and had seen nearly three years' service
in France. Private **Arthur Gilks** (also referred
to as Albert) was with the 11th Battalion Royal
Warwickshire Regiment and died in France on
the 27th January, aged 19. **William McCousins,**
who before joining up had been a gardener for
Mr Dudley Docker, died from pneumonia in a
Casualty Clearing Station on the 12th February.
He was a private with the 5th Battalion Royal
Warwickshire Regiment Labour Corps.

William McCousins

Life in Kenilworth during the early months of 1918 was proving
increasingly difficult. Nine inches of snow fell on Wednesday, 16th
January with a further inch the following day. This was the greatest
depth of snow the town had experienced for many years. It was the
provision of food, however, which was causing even more problems
and required drastic action.

Food Rationing

Early in January, Lord Rhondda, the Minister of Food, recommended
a new scheme of local rationing to prevent queues and provide a fairer
division of foodstuffs for everyone. He suggested that every customer
should be registered with one shop for the purchase of a particular
foodstuff and not be allowed to buy it elsewhere, whilst the shopkeeper
would be required to divide his weekly supplies in fair proportion
amongst all the customers registered with him. The Kenilworth Food
Control Committee decided to evolve their own scheme for rationing
in the town so that as soon as the Food Ministry gave its sanction it
could be set into motion without any delay.

At first the local committees only had to deal with the rationing
of butter, margarine and tea with the maximum weekly allowances
being 4 ounces of margarine or butter and 1½ ounces of tea. Ration
cards were issued for the retailer to mark up each week as the holder
purchased supplies.

One food shortage causing great concern in the town was that of
meat, and it was felt that a meat-rationing scheme should also be
introduced. This shortage had come about because both the butchers

and the public had ignored the Food Control Committee's suggested rationing allowances in December 1917, with the butchers selling, and most people buying, just as usual. This inevitably led to a depletion of the reserves and a resulting curtailment of supplies.

During the second week of January, residents were asked to do as well as they could on the very small quantity that was available. The total supply would be $3/4$ lb per head for a week.

Two weeks later, however, the Kenilworth Food Control Committee had no option but to introduce their own temporary local meat rationing scheme as some inhabitants were still not getting their fair share of meat. Posters with full instructions were printed and tickets delivered to every householder. With each family having a single ticket, it was possible to ensure that everyone obtained meat from only one butcher, once a week. However, it was not possible to fix a uniform rate of meat per head because of the fluctuating supplies; instead, the varying weekly quantities were to be posted in the butchers' shops. This local scheme continued until the national meat scheme came into force in April, when a coupon system displaced the local card system and, instead of working on a weight basis, each coupon had a cash value of 1s 10d worth of meat per head per week.

The Kenilworth Food Control Committee reported after a week or so that the meat scheme had worked most satisfactorily, and beyond expectation. However, by the middle of March they received a petition signed by 151 local working men, which stated

> *We the undersigned workers, beg to petition the Food Control Committee of Kenilworth to grant us a larger proportion of butcher's meat as it is impossible for us to do the heavy work that we are doing on such a small allowance. Our strength is exhausted long before the day's work is finished. This matter is urgent, and we hope it will receive prompt attention.*

The committee replied that it was impossible to give working men extra rations, but by now the government was already considering supplementary rations for heavy workers, having realised the need to keep the workforce healthy. Within a few days the local Food Office was instructed to receive applications from heavy workers for extra rations of meat. By the end of March it was reported that the rationing scheme seemed to be settling down into a smooth working whole.

The last letter from postman James Harris

James Harris returned to the front after home leave in November 1917. Since the beginning of the war he had kept Kenilworth informed of events at the front. He had experienced many battles with the South Staffs Regiment during more than three years service, leaving his post only three times—to convalesce from his wounds at Ypres in 1914 and for two short periods of leave at home. He wrote once more to his wife on the 2nd February 1918 to say that he was due to stay in the trenches for four more days. He was killed in action the following day.

The news of his death was confirmed by a comrade, who found a money order for Mrs Harris in her husband's coat, which he sent on to her. Private Harris, who was 34 years old, left three children, the oldest being only seven years old. He is buried in the British Extension of the Metz-en-Couture Communal Cemetery in France.

The same week, another Kenilworth wife heard better news. Mrs Timms, of Mill End, received a cheering card from her husband Private J. D. Timms of the Coldstream Guards who was captured at Cambrai in November 1917, and held prisoner in Germany. He wrote: 'Just a card to let you know I am well, and being treated well, and when the war is over shall come back to you.' Despite his claim of good treatment, he also told of shortages within the prison camp and asked to be sent parcels of chocolate, milk tablets, oats, jam, Oxo, cheese, tobacco and soap.

Kenilworth Red Cross Hospital

The third anniversary of the opening of the Red Cross Hospital took place in February and was celebrated by a progressive whist drive. The patients had been busy since the New Year and in return for all the entertainment that had been put on for their benefit, had produced their own pantomime. This was *Aladdin* written by Private G. Alderson of the 1st Artists Rifles. It contained many novel features which caused hearty laughter amongst the audience, particularly the second scene, where Aladdin appeared in the trenches, and searching for the lamp, entered the brigadier's dug-out in mistake for a cave and stole his one and only stove. The pantomime proved so popular that a further performance was put on for the public and over 100 attended.

The wounded soldiers also held an exhibition at the Kenilworth Institute of fancy needlework, a skill they had been taught by Miss Eva

Barwell. They produced many original designs, although regimental themes were always their favourites. There were 36 exhibits from 15 exhibitors. Only a few examples were on sale and these were soon snapped up as the majority of the men wanted to keep their handiwork as a reminder of their spell at Kenilworth Hospital.

During February 1918 the vicar of St Nicholas' church, the Rev. J. W. Dennis began to think about a memorial for the dead and wrote the following letter in the parish magazine:

> *I think we should all like to do something to perpetuate the memories of our dead men and boys who have given their lives for their country. Many of us would like to see some beautiful memorial of these gallant lives, so sacred to those who knew and loved them, in our Parish Church. I suggest that we might do something that would both commemorate our dead worthily, and adorn the House of God. Nothing is too beautiful for our Parish Church. We want it to exemplify all that is best in devotion, in knowledge, and in art. Here is a suggestion: The west wall of the church is very bare, and needs enrichment. Might we not have some beautiful picture painted on this wall which would set forth the great Sacrifice into which these men have entered; and then underneath a tablet containing all their names? If this idea appeals to you I think it would be well to start a fund for this purpose as soon as possible, so as to carry out the scheme when the war is over.*

A Kenilworth sailor lost his life in early March 1918. Stoker **Ernest Ashmore** had been transferred to the submarine service and drowned in H.M. Submarine H5 in the Irish Sea on the 2nd March. The

Stoker Ernest Ashmore

submarine was based at Donegal Bay and was patrolling the Irish Sea when she was struck by an unidentified vessel, possibly a British merchant ship, and sank immediately with the loss of all on board. Ernest was 36 years old. His wife Lucy, who lived with her parents Mr and Mrs David Green at 50 Spring Lane, Kenilworth, had already lost one brother, Leonard, in 1917 and another, Arthur, was killed later in 1918. All three are commemorated on Kenilworth war memorial and Ernest is also named on the Portsmouth Naval Memorial.

The German Spring Offensive

On the 21st March 1918, the Germans launched their spring offensive against the Fifth and Third Army in the Somme area. Early in the morning under a cover of dense fog, a bombardment by 6,000 guns opened up on the British positions on a 40-mile front. Over a million shells rained down on the British lines and whole trenches and battalions disappeared without trace. Mixed in with the high explosives was gas, which in the fog was impossible to detect. The bombardment was followed by an infantry attack and the Fifth Army's front virtually collapsed. Some 200,000 were killed or wounded and 90,000 Allied soldiers were taken prisoner. The Germans advanced 14 miles in four days — their greatest gain since the stalemate of 1914.

Six Kenilworth men were killed in the first phase of the spring offensive. Four of them were with the Royal Warwickshire Regiment: Private **Edward Barker** of Dunn's Pit Farm, Private **Charles Silvester Burton** of High Street, Private **Richard Henry Harris** of St John's Street and Lance Corporal **James Drew** of Common Lane.

James Drew (who was also known as Jim) was aged 22, the eldest son of Mr Eli and Mrs Emily Drew. His father was the head gardener for Dudley Docker at The Gables, Kenilworth and the family lived in the Gables Cottage in Common Lane. Jim was born in Solihull and had been head choirboy at St Alphege, Solihull's parish church, before the family moved to Kenilworth. He was very keen on photography, and was a talented artist, both in watercolours and in drawing pen and ink cartoons. Before the war he worked in Coventry as a clerk and was engaged to be married to a Coventry girl.

He joined the Royal Warwickshire Regiment in January 1916 as a signaller with the 10th Battalion. While home on leave in December 1917, *The Kenilworth Advertiser* reported he looked no worse for his experiences. He returned to the front after two weeks.

Corporal James Drew

A letter sent to his mother in March 1918 conveyed his weariness of the war and his longing to return home:

Dearest Mumsie, …. Yes, it has been lovely weather here, just how as you say I used to like it on Sundays. Oh! mum what a change it would be to have one of our dear old Sundays once again now, wouldn't it, for dad could bring us some daffs now couldn't he and we used to love our flowers hadn't we. ….

I expect the dear old Common and the Crackley woods will be all starting to bud and the anemones will soon be out and the primroses won't they and the daffs in the kitchen garden. ….

It will soon be Easter, I wish I could have come over, so that we could have gone to Church dear in the morning but distance makes no difference does it we are all together in Spirit aren't we. This is Passion Sunday today and next Sunday, Palm Sunday. The palm is all out here. …

Jim never made Easter. He was killed on March 25th, the day after Palm Sunday. The sad news was relayed to his parents by a comrade and close friend, Private W. E. Armston, who was in the same shell-hole, and removed the letter wallets and a few personal effects from the body to return to Jim's parents. Private Armston was himself severely wounded and after the action, Jim's body was never found.

Official Notification of Death

It took several weeks for the official information to be sent to his parents. The official letter, sent to the next of kin of all those who fell, was sent on May 2nd (reproduced on the opposite page) together with a formal message of sympathy from the King and Queen.

Jim Drew has no known grave, and is commemorated on the Arras Memorial in France. He is also honoured on a memorial at St Alphege's church, Solihull, in the Oddfellows Hall, Leamington, and in the City of Coventry Book to the Fallen, in the Memorial Park in Coventry, the city where he worked.

His mother never got over his death and would walk across Kenilworth twice a week from her home at The Common with flowers to place at the War Memorial in Abbey End. When she herself died Jim's medals were buried with her.

Jim was the uncle of Kenilworth local historian John Drew.

No. _____

(If replying. please
quote above No.)

ARMY FORM B. 104—82.

Infantry Record Office,

WARWICK

2 - MAY. 1918   191

Sir.

It is my painful duty to inform you that a report has been received from the War Office notifying the death of :—

(No.) *16230.*   (Rank) *Private.*

(Name) *James Drew.*

(Regiment) *10ᵗʰ* ROYAL WARWICKSHIRE REGT.

which occurred *with the Ex. Force. France.*

on the *25ᵗʰ March 1918.*

The report is to the effect that he *was killed in action.*

By His Majesty's command I am to forward the enclosed message of sympathy from Their Gracious Majesties the King and Queen. I am at the same time to express the regret of the Army Council at the soldier's death in his Country's service.

I am to add that any information that may be received as to the soldier's burial will be communicated to you in due course. A separate leaflet dealing more fully with this subject is enclosed.

I am,

Sir.

Your obedient Servant,

H.C. Foster

Lt.   Lt-Col.

Officer in charge of Records.

i/c Infantry Records,
No. 7 DISTRICT.

18540. Wt. 5529/M 2529. 150M. 7/17. R. & L., Ltd. Forms B 104—82/2.

The Official Notification of the Death of Private James Drew

Two others were killed in this initial phase. Trooper **William Beevers** aged 20, lived at Newlands, Waverley Road and was with the Queen's Own Oxfordshire Hussars.

Sapper **Charles Harold Clifft**, who was known by his second name Harold, was 25, a Mounted Sapper with the Royal Engineers and the eldest son of Mr and Mrs Clifft of Malthouse Lane.

Harold was engaged to be married to May Lovell a servant to the vicar of St Nicholas' church. May and her sister had moved to Kenilworth from

Sapper Charles Harold Clifft

Somerset with the previous vicar, the Rev. Cairns. She met Harold in Kenilworth and they became engaged. Harold was reported missing on March 23rd 1918 and it was a month later that his parents heard that he had been killed in action on that day.

His brother Ernest, also a sapper, was in hospital with a broken leg at that time but he survived the war. Harold's fiancée May returned to Somerset after he was killed. He was buried in the Grand-Seraucourt British Cemetery in France.

Two Kenilworth men who survived the war gained military honours in March 1918. Sergeant Walter Askew received the Distinguished Conduct Medal and Private George Sheepy, the Military Medal.

A second phase of the German's attack was launched on the 9th April 1918. This was on the twelve-mile front between Armentières and La Bassée and once again the attack was preceded with a massive bombardment before the German infantry went in.

By the 12th April, Field Marshal Sir Douglas Haig had thrown his last troops into the battle without preventing the Germans advancing. It was a desperate moment causing Haig to issue the following statement to his troops:

With our backs to the wall and believing in the justice of our cause each one must fight on to the end. The safety of our homes and the freedom of mankind alike depend upon the conduct of each one of us at

*this critical moment. There is no other course open to us but to fight it
out. Every position must be held to the last man.*

A further three Kenilworth men were killed in this second phase of the
Spring Offensive. Private **Charles William Newey**, aged 38, a married
man, whose parents lived in New Row, was reported missing on the
17th April and presumed killed on this day when no further news was
heard of him. He was with the 2nd Battalion Worcestershire Regiment
and is commemorated on the Ploegsteert memorial.

Private **William Henry Grainger**, aged 26, is commemorated on the
same memorial. He was killed in action on the 13th April serving with
the 14th battalion Royal Warwickshire Regiment.

Private **Ernest Hopkins**, also aged 26, was killed in action serving
with the 3rd Battalion Coldstream Guards near Armentières on the
13th April. He lived in Henry Street, Kenilworth with his parents and
was brother to the two sisters who died in the Lusitania disaster. Ernest
had joined the army in March 1915 and had been in the battles of the
Somme and at Cambrai.

On the 29th April the Germans made their final effort, again
beginning with a massive bombardment and gas shells followed by
the infantry. A combined Anglo-French force however stopped them
by unexpectedly concentrated heavy fire and, although the Germans
made a few small gains, the expected breakthrough never occurred.
The Kenilworth Advertiser contained many reports of the heavy fighting
in France during the spring months of 1918 including new thrusts by
the Germans and British withdrawals, as well as the capture of many
British prisoners by the Germans.

Recruitment continues at home

Military tribunals continued to be held and a new order was received
that gave men refused permission to appeal by the local tribunal, the
right to get a decision from an Appeals Tribunal.

One such case involved Frederick Hobbins of 35 Albion Street whose
appeal was allowed when it was realised that he had incorrectly been
described as a fellmonger's labourer and not as a fellmonger's skinner
which was a protected occupation.

At a further tribunal Mr William Moss applied for conditional
exemption for his brother Fred Moss, aged 45 and married, of High
Street, Kenilworth. He told the tribunal that his business of a grocer

had been run pre-war with a staff of six, but now was carried on only by himself, his brother and a boy of 15; it would be impossible to serve the large number of persons registered with him were his brother taken, and he would have no alternative but to close. The committee gave him two months to find and train a substitute for his brother.

The weather in Kenilworth at Easter 1918 was very cold and miserable preventing the usual Easter influx of holidaymakers. There were many cases of whooping cough in the town, causing the Kenilworth Infants' Welfare Centre to temporarily stop its weekly meetings, which were held in the Wesleyan Church school room.

The allotments were getting off to a very late start but gardeners were reminded of the season of 1917 when strong growth in May more than made up for a very late start, and they were urged to set late varieties of potatoes and main crops of carrots at this time.

By Whitsun, as predicted, the weather improved and thousands of Coventry people descended on Kenilworth for the Monday Bank Holiday. Nightingales were reported at Knowle Hill and Villiers Hill at the end of May, after their numbers had been sadly depleted in the previous two years.

Blight had been affecting a lot of flowers and fruit in the town, and there was also a report of a plague of green caterpillars devouring hedges of white thorn, devastating orchards and giving great oak trees a gaunt and unpleasant look. Along the Coventry-Kenilworth Road, in particular, these caterpillars were reported making great inroads into the foliage of the trees, and hanging over the footpaths in tangled festoons of webs and green grubs. Gardeners were strongly advised to spray their orchards.

At the beginning of June news was received of the death of Private **Arthur Henry Spicer** the son of Mr Arthur Spicer, plumber and painter, of Warwick Road. Private Spicer had died from bronchial pneumonia at Turin, Italy on the 25th May. He had joined the 2nd Warwickshire Regiment two years earlier but, not being constitutionally strong, had had several attacks of illness, which kept him in England until autumn 1917 when he went out to France, and in November was sent to Italy. He was 32 years old and worked in his father's business as a plumber, painter and signwriter.

In France, although German losses had been high in the Spring offensive, Ludendorff launched further offensives with the usual devastating bombardment followed by massed infantry attacks. British and French losses were high, and many prisoners were taken, although by now American troops were arriving in substantial numbers.

Two Kenilworth people experienced the massive German bombing at close quarters while they were in hospitals in France.

Mrs Isobel Higginson (youngest daughter of the late Mr Charles Robertson of Abbey End) wrote to her mother the day following the bombing attack, 'Am quite safe, after a very trying night'—intimating that the hospital in France where she was working was the scene of an attack. She had lost her husband, a lieutenant in the Lancashire Fusiliers, early in the war and had returned to her profession as a nurse and been on hospital duty in France for over two years.

Private **Harry Stanley**, of High Street, Kenilworth, with the Royal Warwickshire Regiment, was also at a base hospital in France which suffered massive bombing by the Germans. Although he and all the men in his ward escaped injury, there were several deaths and many were injured. He was brought back to England but later died in the Ministry of Pensions Hospital, Leicester on the 5th September 1923. He was 43 years old.

Further casualties at this time were Corporal **Harry Lloyd Bidmead** of the 16th Battalion Lancashire Fusiliers who was killed in action by a shell on the 6th June, Private **Walter Cannon** of Barrow Road, with the 6th Battalion Dorsetshire Regiment, who died on the 8th June, and Sergeant **Alfred Nixon**, a staff sergeant with the Royal Field Artillery, killed on 17th July.

Harry Lloyd Bidmead, who had joined up at the beginning of the war, had seen continuous service, writing home in 1916 describing the terrible trench bombardment he was having to endure. In June 1918, his sister, Mrs Buckingham of Mount Pleasant, Albion Street, received a letter from his lieutenant informing her that Harry had been killed in France. Corporal Bidmead was in charge of a platoon in the trenches when a shell fell on them and killed him instantly. He was 23 years of age. Prior to the war he had been a plumber for Mr J. H. Lawrence, builder, of Warwick Road.

Corporal Harry Bidmead

Alfred Nixon was 38 years old, a married man from High Street, Kenilworth, and father of two small boys. He had been in Canada at the outbreak of the war and had immediately joined the artillery. He was an instructor in England until January 1918 when he went to France. In a letter to his wife the regimental chaplain wrote, 'It is also a comfort to know that he suffered but little. Help was near. The doctor lived within a few yards, and a field ambulance was ready at hand. He did not suffer like to so many poor soldiers do when wounded. I took the funeral service, which was most reverent and solemn. Nearly the whole of the Headquarters Staff were there with an officer and the Regimental Sergt-Major.' Sergeant Nixon is buried in Nine Elms British Cemetery at Poperinghe.

More and more aeroplanes were being brought into the war at this stage and many recruits now joined the Royal Air Force. One of these was **H. G. R. Boyt** who had moved from Leamington to live at Charlton, Windy Arbour in 1917, joining the RAF in the autumn of that year. He was gazetted as a Second Lieutenant early in 1918 and was completing his aerial gunnery course before going to France when his plane crashed and he was instantly killed. Before joining the Air Force he had been employed at the engineering company BTH (British Thompson Houston) Rugby. He was buried in All Saints churchyard, Stanhoe, Norfolk.

Prisoner of War Fund

By July 1918, the number of known Kenilworth men being held prisoner had risen to fourteen and, because of the need for a wider appeal for funds, the Prisoner of War Fund was now registered under the War Charities Act of 1916. The balance sheet for the half year showed receipts and expenditures of £162 7s 8d, with the majority of the money collected in boxes in various hotels and clubs throughout the town. Three food parcels were being sent to each prisoner every fortnight, together with bread made locally in Copenhagen and Berne, at a total estimated cost of 17s 6d per prisoner per week.

There were several men known to be prisoners at the time whose cases had yet to be officially notified. One of these was Private **Harry Manton** of Spring Lane, who was 22 years old and married. He was taken prisoner in March 1918 and died at Valenciennes on the 29th August 1918.

Others to die this summer included 19-year old Private **John Stanley**, one of four brothers from Bulkington Cottages who was killed in action on 3rd August. He was the second brother to be killed with another honourably discharged as disabled.

Private **Spencer Walton**, also aged 19, from Windy Arbour, had been in France for five months with the Royal Suffolk Regiment when he died on the 23rd August.

With the war now entering its fifth year, services were held in all the local churches. St Nicholas' church had a procession of 150 representatives of the different public bodies who paraded to the church where the vicar, Rev. Joseph W. Dennis asked the congregation to 'not lose faith because the war is so protracted.'

Food shortages

Food continued to be rationed at home and, because of meat shortages, many Kenilworth folk had started to keep rabbits. *The Kenilworth Advertiser* considered that the number of rabbits being kept in Kenilworth during the summer months of 1918 was quite extraordinary and reported many people with 30 to 50 rabbits who were still increasing their hutches and stocks.

During August 1918 the local council decided to abandon the idea of establishing a communal kitchen in the town. It was felt that, although the idea for most towns was excellent, for Kenilworth it was different because of its scattered and open nature. They realized that people would be unwilling to travel the mile which separated the three extreme parts of the town from its centre to patronise a communal kitchen, particularly in hot or inclement weather. As a weekly taking of £15 at least would be necessary to pay expenses they saw the probability of loss and decided to abandon the idea.

Autumn brought the usual bumper crop of blackberries and schoolchildren were again given special holidays for picking. This time adults as well as children were paid to pick and 3d a pound was paid for the blackberries which were taken to St Nicholas' School where there was a packing depot.

The harvest of crops in 1918 proved to be a record one—the best since 1868—but there were problems because of the shortage of harvest workers. Help was given by soldiers who had returned from the army as unfit, together with gangs of German prisoners and large numbers of women. These were land girls as well as part-time women workers, but still more help was needed and a call went out nationally for further strong healthy girls and women to help with the threshing.

The Threshing Sub-committee asked the Warwickshire War Agricultural Committee to raise a minimum of 300 girls for this work. The idea was to share the limited supply of skilled men so that each threshing machine was worked by three men supported by six women. The majority of the girls required were sought from the large centres of industrial population including Birmingham and Coventry and were to be billeted in various villages to work on nearby farms.

Haig's Forces break the Hindenberg Line

In France, Colonel Haig launched a series of major assaults which culminated on the 29th September with the breaking of the Hindenburg line. By the 8th October there were over a million Americans in the battle area and the numbers were still pouring in. A second army was created on 10th October and both were almost continuously in action. Casualties on both sides were high including ten Kenilworth men killed in action in September and October.

Private Edward George **Webster**, of White's Row, who had been a choirboy at St John's Church, and was with the 2nd Hampshire Regiment, was killed in action at Avrincourt on the 13th September. Private **George Henry Frazer**, whose brother Ernest had been killed the previous year, was reported missing on the 21st September. He was with the 7th Royal West Kent Regiment and his body was never found. Before enlistment he was employed at the Kenilworth Tannery.

Private Edward Webster

An assistant church organist and chorister at St Nicholas' church, Private **William E. Eales**, was killed in action on the 22nd September. He was a married man, aged 31, with a young daughter and lived in Waverley Road. Prior to the war, he had worked in the local railway goods office and later with the Rover Company in Coventry. He was drafted in February 1917 to the Army Ordnance Corps, but later transferred to the Duke of Cornwall's Light Infantry, being sent to

France after a short training. He had not long been in the trenches when he was killed.

The Sunday after hearing the sad news, the members of the choir placed a wreath on his choir stall. The vicar paid a tribute to him in his sermon and at the conclusion of the evening service, in place of the usual organ recital the organist played the 'Dead March'.

A former member of the Kenilworth Voluntary Training Corps, Private **Albert Edward Dilworth**, from New Row, was killed in action on the 25th September. He first joined the Royal Warwickshire Regiment but was later transferred to the Manchester Regiment. He was 19 years old and his only brother, Corporal Ernest Dilworth, had been a prisoner of war for two years at this time. His parents received the following letter of sympathy in the loss of their son:

Private Albert Dilworth

….. Pte. A. E. Dilworth was well known both to his Platoon officers and myself as a thoroughly trustworthy and zealous soldier. It will be some consolation to you to know that in the act wherein he died he was seeking the greater safety of others. He had just removed a box of bombs to a place less likely in his opinion to be struck by enemy fire when he was killed immediately by a shell of great calibre which exploded and blew in the trench, this during a very intense bombardment. Neither the rifle, equipment, nor any other effects of Pte. Dilworth could be recovered. He had necessarily died before he was even aware of the injury.

Upon the evening of the same day (he was killed about 3.15 a.m.), Sept 26, I saw Pte. Dilworth interred in the trench he had so gallantly defended—a trench which not thereafter was nor ever again will be used. I said the prayers from the Burial Service of the Church of England, as nearly as I could recall them, in the presence of Sec.-Lieut. Peregrine, Sergt. Huddart, and members of his platoon. The officers, N.C.O.'s and men of the Platoon, including myself, extend their deepest sympathy.—Faithfully yours, J. C. Whitebrook.

Private **Albert Buckingham** of the 10th Battalion Royal Warwickshire Regiment was reported missing on the 25th September and presumed

Sgt Charles James Martin   *Private Arthur Green*   *Private Harvey Warren*

dead as no further news of him was received.

Sergeant **Charles James Martin**, aged 22, a Kenilworth postman, was killed in action on the 14th October. He was with the 34th Battalion Machine Gun Corps.

Private **Arthur Green**, the youngest son of Mr and Mrs D. Green, of Spring Lane, was killed outright on the 22nd October when a shell fell on a post held by him and four other men. He was also with the 10th Battalion Royal Warwickshire Regiment; he had joined up in 1916 when he was 18 years old and had been in France for six months.

On reporting Arthur Green's death, *The Kenilworth Advertiser* remarked upon how heavily the little locality of a score of houses in Spring Lane had suffered in the war:

> .... *Besides these two boys of Mr Green there are Pte. Jim Tookey, Pte. Vic Gardner, and Pte. John Garratt amongst the killed; Pte. Flowers, Butler, Stock and Manton, prisoners; and one man, Pte. Martin, maimed. In the adjoining street–Henry Street–there are six families mourning men lost in the war, viz. Pte. J. Whateley, Pte. J. Harris, Pte. Watson, Pte. Letts, Pte. Jack Collett, and Pte. Ernest Hopkins.*

A further member of the 10th Battalion Royal Warwickshire Regiment, Sergeant **Arthur Lake**, was killed in action on the 21st October. He had been on active service throughout the war and had previously been wounded three times.

Private **Harvey Warren**, from Clinton Lane was killed in action on the 28th October. He was 36 years old, a married man with three children under seven years of age and was with the 2nd South

Lancashire Regiment. He joined up in June 1915 and went out to France in October 1915 seeing continuous service with only two home leaves. Before the war he was an insurance agent with the Prudential Assurance Company.

One soldier, Private **Frederick Daniel Mulcahy** died from wounds at a casualty clearing station in France on the 25th October. He was 36 years old and with the 12th/13th Battalion Northumberland Fusiliers.

Spanish Flu

Private Frederick Mulcahy

Three further Kenilworth men who died that autumn succumbed to influenza. An extraordinary epidemic of influenza, which became known as 'Spanish Flu', although it seemed to have originated in China or perhaps India, was sweeping across the world. It was very virulent and caused over 2,000 deaths a week in London alone.

Captain **Sacheverel Darwin Wilmot**, aged 33, and son of Rev. and Mrs Darwin Wilmot of Castle Hill, Kenilworth, died of influenza in Karachi Military Hospital on the 14th October. He had been educated at Rugby School and The King's School, Macclesfield, where his father was headmaster for 25 years. Captain Wilmot received his commission and joined the Royal Garrison Artillery in 1904. He was in England on leave at the outbreak of the war and rejoined his battery in India, spending part of his service in the middle east where he took part in the capture of Baghdad, and was in command of a heavy battery in other operations. He was twice mentioned in despatches and in August 1916 received the Serbian Order of the White Eagle. He was married with three children. As well as being commemorated on Kenilworth War Memorial, Captain Wilmot is also named on memorials at Rugby School and The King's School, Macclesfield.

Bombardier **Charles Howard Gregory,** with the Royal Field Artillery, also died of influenza in Wimereux Hospital on the 24th October. He was 24 years old, lived in School Lane, and before the war had been employed as a clerk at Kenilworth Railway station. Likewise, ex-Sergeant **Henry Oliver Edmond**, the eldest son of the late Mr Edmond, manager of Kenilworth Gas Works, died of influenza at Coventry after only three days' illness. Oliver had seen nearly three years service in the Royal Army Medical Corps in France before being discharged. He was 28 when he died and was buried in Kenilworth Cemetery.

At this stage the town of Kenilworth had escaped a severe influenza epidemic with the schools and other public places operating as usual, although in a neighbouring town one large school at least was closed. By the middle of November, however, deaths from influenza within the town were increasing with six deaths in one week, including Oliver Edmond's only child, a baby boy of eight months.

The Town Clerk was ordered to obtain 1,500 pamphlets related to the prevention of the disease and have them distributed to every house in the town.

The End of the War

In France the stage was now set for the final assault. On the 2nd November *The Kenilworth Advertiser* reported that the British, French and American armies were moving forward steadily on practically the whole of the battle front from the neighbourhood of Ghent to north of Verdun. On the Valenciennes-Le Cateau line the British had secured another 1000 prisoners making 10,000 since the attack began and had pushed their advance south of Valenciennes, against determined opposition. The First American Army was continuing to make excellent headway on the Verdun front, where in a month they had inflicted severe losses on the enemy on this 25 mile line, taken 20,000 prisoners, 150 guns and 1000 trench mortars.

By now news of the collapse of Germany was coming in steadily. On the 8th November there were riots in Munich and in other German towns on the following day. Finally, at 5.00 a.m. on 11th November 1918 an Armistice was signed with Germany in a railway carriage in the Forest of Compiègne. The news of this momentous event was relayed as rapidly as possible throughout the warring armies, and at 11.00 a.m. on the same day the guns were silenced.

Kenilworth receives the news

A rumour began to spread around the town from about 10.00 a.m. on the 11th November that the armistice had been signed and this was later confirmed. Mr Randall immediately had the tannery bell rung and the fire horn blown. Flags came fluttering out of windows for the first time since 1914, streamers across streets were added, and gradually the whole town took on a gala appearance. The church bells rang for a short spell before the 12 o'clock service, at which quite a number of worshippers attended, and afterwards the bells were pealing throughout the day at intervals. There was a calmness, however, in the way that Kenilworth received the joyful news. As *The Kenilworth Advertiser* described it:

> *There was no parading and shouting, just an isolated cheer here and there when the news was first broken. The feelings of the masses were too deep for 'Mafiking'. Four years of anxiety and shortages, four years of recurrent sorrow and sense of loss, four years of uphill battle against adversity and in face at times of actual defeat, had rubbed away the will to unrestrained merrymaking. Rather a feeling of solemn thanksgiving pervaded, and when at eventide the bells of the Parish Church announced another service steps turned that way, and there assembled a crowded congregation.*

The following day at a meeting of the Kenilworth Urban District Council, Mr Randall, the chairman, spoke of the long-looked-for peace that had come to them at last and he hoped the menace of militarism had now gone for ever. It seemed incredible to him that a nation of peaceful people should have turned out in the space of one or two years an army in millions fit to cope with the best legions the Kaiser could command, and not only that, but to prove more than a match for them. He was proud to report that 836 young men from Kenilworth had joined up since the outbreak of hostilities, although out of that number he was sorry to say 90 had made the supreme sacrifice. The joy bells were ringing practically all over the country and he was sure that everyone was delighted and proud and thankful that they had lived to see the day of peace, and that this wicked war had come to an end. 'May we never have another war,' he concluded. 'We hope this will be the last war of the world.'

Chapter 7

Kenilworth after the War

The Great War lasted for 1,500 days, with 67 million men in uniform, of whom 8.5 million were killed and half the rest wounded. Four million died on the Western Front. In total, Britain and its Empire suffered 3.2 million casualties, including a million dead. The 30 battalions of the Royal Warwickshire Regiment lost 11,610 men.

Even these numbers were dwarfed by the natural disaster of Spanish influenza which swept the world in the winter of 1918, killing an estimated 40 million, including a quarter of a million in Britain.

The end of the war was not the signal for immediate demobilisation of the army, nor did it mark the end of military deaths. Soldiers continued to suffer accidents and illnesses on duty from which some died, others wounded in action lingered in hospital or were released with disabilities from which they never recovered.

Private **William Jakeman**, aged 22, of Arthur Street, was the first Kenilworth man to die after the war, as the result of an accidental shell explosion on November 22nd. He is buried at Cambrai in France.

Our men begin to arrive home

As the months passed, the men began returning to England, and the focus of the story changes from those who gave their lives to those who survived and returned to find their lives would never be the same.

The first prisoner of war to arrive in Kenilworth in early December 1918 was Corporal Ernest Dilworth of New Row, the brother of Albert Dilworth who had died in the last month of the war. Corporal Dilworth had been captured unharmed on July 18th 1916 and spent two years in camps in Germany. On his return he talked about the shortage of food and the lifeline of food parcels from home, all but two of which reached him.

He was followed in mid-December by Privates Stock, Flowers, and Butler of Spring Lane, Private Atkins who lived in Coventry, Private George Sheepy of High Street, Private William Gregory of School Lane, and Private Arthur Bird of Warwick Road. There was also news of George Sheepy's brother, Sergeant Walter Sheepy, who was hoping to get home in time for Christmas.

The Sheepy family at war:
top row: Sergeant Judd (brother-in-law), Sergeant Walter Sheepy
bottom row: Privates William, George, and Driver Owen Sheepy.

The Sheepy family were especially blessed. Mrs Sheepy of High Street was proud of her boys. Four out of five of her sons had joined up as volunteers early in the war, together with her daughter's husband, Harry Judd, who served in Italy. All of them were to return.

Private William Sheepy joined up at the beginning of the war and was wounded at the Battle of the Somme in 1916. His brother George also joined in 1914 but was too young to go to the front at the time. He was sent into action in May 1916 and was shot through the head at the Battle of the Somme on July 19th. He was captured and his eye removed by a German doctor. He was a prisoner in France, Germany and eventually Switzerland, before being released on December 6th 1918, arriving home just six days later on December 12th. He was awarded the Military Medal for gallantry.

Young Owen Sheepy lived safely through two years of service in France as a driver.

Sergeant Walter Sheepy served for three and a half years, being wounded on four occasions before being captured on March 21st 1918. Despite hopes for an early release, the family reunion had to wait until his return in mid-January 1919.

Once home, the men told their stories of imprisonment and treatment at the hands of the Germans. Some had experienced rough treatment, others had fared better, but many spoke of the lack of food and the withholding of Red Cross food parcels. Their hunger was never fully appeased. Private George Sheepy received just three of many parcels sent to him, one from the Prisoners of War Fund, one from his mother, and one from his sister. Loaves of bread often had to be thrown away because they had gone bad. Arthur Bird, who was captured on the 24th March 1918 at Ypres, lost 4 stone in weight. Though numerous parcels had been sent to him, he never received a single one.

1919

Closure of the Kenilworth Red Cross Hospital

The Red Cross Hospital in the Parochial Hall celebrated New Year 1919 with a party and entertainment. The event also doubled as its closing ceremony. During the evening, the patients received presents, the matron, Mrs W. G. Blatch, was presented with a silver rose bowl, and certificates of merit from the Red Cross Society were handed out to Dr Growse and the other workers. Dr Growse spoke of the work of the hospital, which, since February 1915, had accepted 967 patients for treatment. By the 11th of January all the remaining soldiers had gone and, after auctioning off the surplus articles of furniture, equipment and bed linen, the work of the Kenilworth Red Cross Hospital was brought to a close. Dr Growse lived but a few months more, passing away on the 19th of July at the age of 64.

Kenilworth soldier Private **William Ward**, of St John's Street, died in hospital on the 26th February, aged 19 years. After being at the front with the 2nd Hampshire Regiment for only a few weeks, he was badly wounded at Ypres in September 1918 and transferred to the Cambridge Hospital at Aldershot. He is buried in Kenilworth Cemetery.

Appeals for funds

The year 1919 saw a succession of public subscriptions sought from the people of Kenilworth. An appeal for £1,200 to support the costs of the St Nicholas' Church living was answered by a donation of £250 from Dudley Docker, with £100 each from Miss Wilson, Miss Evans, Mr Percy Martin and Mr Kevitt Rotherham, £50 from Mr W. Mitchell and £25 from Mr S. Keeling and Messrs G. M. Turner, A. W. Street, F. Phelps, H. Quick. When the total of £1,141 14s was announced on January 11th, Dudley Docker suggested that donors double their amount as an offering to celebrate the peace.

As the servicemen returned home, it became apparent that the Working Men's Club in Albion Street was too small and three cottages and vacant land opposite Albion Tavern were purchased for expansion. However, a more suitable property came on the market in the shape of Montague House in Rosemary Hill; it was bought by Mr Randall for £2,200 and leased to the Club for 14 years with an option to purchase at any time.

KENILWORTH **WORKING MENS CLUB & INSTITUTE.**
COMMITTEE 1919

A ROWE.   J. FAXON   J. W WARD   B. LOWE   C. HOLMES.   G JAMES.   F. FLOWERS.
J. SEWELL.   A. NASON   C. MOSELEY   A. FRANKLIN   F. BARNWELL   F. BASTOCK.   S. LATRE.
G. PETTIFOR.   T. SHERWIN   C. RANDALL   T. J. MASON.   H. ROWEN.

In addition to supporting the Working Men's Club, Mr Randall, the manager of the Tannery was also the Chairman of the Town Council and Chairman of the Kenilworth Conservative Club. He had recently moved house to Abbotsfield, which he purchased together with the cottages in Little Virginia from Lincoln Chandler, who moved away on business. In February, his name was put forward for the County Council as an independent and, with support from the Working Men's Club and the Conservative Club, he was elected unopposed.

By March, the membership of the Working Men's Club had increased from 150 to 400 and a Victory Brass Band was formed. St John's Cricket Club re-opened and an Angling Club was started. A Victory Ball was held at the Parochial Hall and Easter saw a record number of visitors coming to the town and Castle.

The town was returning to some semblance of normality that had been enjoyed in pre-war days. Extensive building plans were being proposed and the County Council planned to erect a new school in School Lane. The brickyards, which had been taken over for Government Stores, were handed back to the owners, but now faced a pumping-out programme estimated to be at least three months before they could be restored to production.

Memorials proposed in the churches of St Nicholas and St John

Around the country, cities, towns and villages were beginning to think of memorials to the dead. In Kenilworth, both St Nicholas' and St John's churches planned to have memorial plaques paid for by local subscription. St Nicholas', being the longest established church in town, decided to commemorate all Kenilworth losses, whether church-goers or not, whilst St John's focused on a more specific memorial to commemorate the 29 members of the parish who had lost their lives. In addition St John's planned new oak panelling in the church around the reredos, and new choir stalls at a total cost of £225.

The project at St Nicholas had begun with a 'Roll of Honour', starting in December 1914 with the following entry in the Parish Magazine:

James Harris, aged 31 years
Sidney Charles Aitken, died October 23rd aged 19 1/2 years
James William Smith, aged 23 years
Frederick H Buswell, died November 10th
Harry Barnett, died October 19th aged 28 years.

All of these were to be listed on the Kenilworth War Memorial, except Private Frederick Buswell, who is almost certainly the grandson of the Parish Clerk, James Buswell. Frederick's father had died and his mother remarried and moved to Farnham in Surrey where, as Mrs Hatch, she was listed by the Commonwealth War Graves Commission as his next of kin. This illustrates the difficulty in establishing an authentic list for the war memorial. There were a number of men linked to Kenilworth who may be commemorated elsewhere, in one or more locations.

Throughout the war, many of the fallen were remembered in services at St Nicholas, and the Church Roll of Honour continued to be updated. By October 1917 the number listed stood at 53 and the vicar appealed for 'any more names that ought to appear on this noble list.' By April 1918, it had grown to 66, but lacked the names of many other Kenilworth men who had died by that time. Other churches had honoured their fallen in various ways and so it was natural that the St Nicholas' Parish Magazine focused on its own.

The call for a permanent memorial in St Nicholas' Church was made in the Parish Magazine on February 1st 1919 by the vicar, the Rev. J. W. Dennis. He suggested that such a memorial be 'in the form of a tablet containing all the names of the men who have made the great sacrifice from this parish' and invited subscriptions to be sent to himself or the churchwardens.

The full list of names for the St Nicholas' Memorial was assembled by the Town Clerk, Mr Hadow, who combined the Church's Roll of Honour with his own list of all who served in the War that he had compiled for the Town Council since 1915. In July 1919, he sent a combined list of 110 names to the *Kenilworth Advertiser* and asked for information about anyone who had been omitted. Three of these 110 did not appear on the St Nicholas Memorial: Arthur Lake, H. P. Rawlings and Kenneth Salt.

Sergeant Lake was the son of a local blacksmith from Albion Street whose death was reported in the local press just before the end of the war. Both parents had died and his sister, as next of kin, lived in Coventry. His name was initially missing from all Kenilworth Memorials, but was added to the Town Memorial at a later date.

Neither H. P. Rawlings nor Kenneth Salt appear on any Kenilworth Memorial. Private Salt may have survived the war. The 1901 Census reveals only one Kenneth Salt in Kenilworth and after the war a man of that name played football in the town before emigrating to Australia.

The design for the St Nicholas' Memorial was proposed by Mr Quick in the form of a plaque in alabaster and marble at a cost of £120. This met with general approval, but the subscriptions to pay for it were slow to build. The month following the announcement, only £10 19s 7d had been collected. Meanwhile, St John's Church had raised £115 0s 11d, including £5 11s 7d from the scholars and children. The response for the St Nicholas' Memorial was disappointing compared with over a thousand pounds collected for the Church living in the previous month. Was this because some were waiting to see what the Town Council would do?

In April 1919, the *Kenilworth Advertiser* commented that some small towns had already erected wayside shrines yet Kenilworth lagged behind. Judged by the slow pace of subscriptions for the St Nicholas' Church Memorial, it was suggested that a significant town memorial might be beyond Kenilworth's resources.

Over the coming months, the church collections slowly achieved their targets, with St Nicholas' reaching the full amount of £120 by November and raising this figure to £128. 9s 7d by December. Meanwhile St John's raised £198.15s by the end of the year.

The Post Office Scroll of Honour

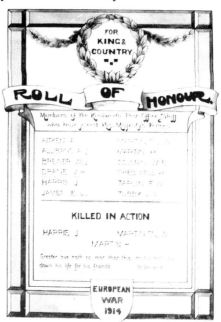

Other organisations began to erect their own memorials. Miss Rivers of Waverley Road presented a hand-written scroll to the Post Office, commemorating the twelve members of staff who had served in the war. This included three postmen who had died: Sergeant Charles J. Martin, Private James Harris and Private Harold Martin. Of these, Private James Harris has featured throughout our narrative through his graphic letters home.

Victor Drane, a post-office clerk survived the war but died at sea of pneumonia on April 23rd, 1919, on his

The Post Office Scroll of Honour

Sapper Victor Drane

way home. This information was inserted on the scroll just beneath his name.

Sapper Drane, the 24-year old son of Mr and Mrs W. Drane of Henry Street, had joined up as a reservist in 1915 as a field telegraphist with the Royal Engineers and saw service in France before going to Mesopotamia. From France he sent home a souvenir – a fuse of an 18-pounder German shell, which burst near him and put ten men out of action. It was a chance shot which fell well beyond the line, amongst some marching infantry.

Back in England, further honours were announced: the DSO was awarded to Lt. Edwin Carter, son of the licensee of The Engine Inn. Company Sergeant Nixon and Sergeant Varney received the DCM, and Sergeant George Hooton the Meritorious Service Medal.

War Memorials around the country

Around the country War Memorials were being discussed in a range of different forms: lists of the fallen, recreation grounds, libraries, hospitals, social clubs, village halls. Some of these were being paid for by public subscription and through the local rates.

The Kenilworth Council sought clarification of the role of public funds in building a memorial and received information from the President of the Local Government Board which was published in *The Kenilworth Advertiser*.

It explained that the Board was aware of a number of local authorities contemplating using money from their rates. It expressed a willingness to allow reasonable expenditure for proposals of a useful character, such as recreation grounds, hospitals or libraries—which were within the statutory powers of local authorities—and others such as village halls or social clubs, which would require authorization from the Board. However, it recommended that a public subscription should be called for before recourse to the rates and that the people should be consulted before any substantial expenditure.

Kenilworth Council seeks ideas for a Town Memorial

On May 13th, 1919, the Town Council discussed the growing desire for Kenilworth to have its own Memorial. It was agreed to have a public meeting at the Drill Hall on Saturday, 24th May, to encourage suggestions from the townsfolk and to appoint a Committee to deal with the War Memorial and the coming Peace Celebrations.

Meanwhile, on Sunday, May 18th, a meeting was called to form a local branch of the newly constituted National Federation of Discharged and Demobilised Sailors & Soldiers (NatFedDDSS), which would later become the British Legion. A new club required an initial fifty members, which proved to be an easy target with the several hundred ex-servicemen in the town. At the meeting more than fifty enrolled, with Mr Ben Walkley of 12 High Street as acting Honorary Secretary. A further meeting was set for May 30th to elect the officers.

In the meantime, the first public meeting to discuss the War Memorial on May 24th was addressed by the Chairman, Councillor Randall, who explained that nothing was 'cut and dried' and that it was up to those present to make suggestions for 'a memorial which should be of a lasting character to be handed down from generation to generation'. The meeting voted unanimously to 'express the willingness for the raising of the necessary funds'.

The Chairman suggested that the Abbey Fields was a lovely site for the memorial and emphasised that the town memorial was entirely independent of those planned by the churches, which he fully supported.

The first suggestion came from Mr A. H. Spicer for a monument in the Abbey Fields inscribed with the names of the fallen. Mrs K. Rotherham suggested a public library.

Lord Ernest Seymour—whose late wife had organised the Red Cross Hospital in the war—suggested a Cottage Hospital.

Mr E. A. Jeacock spoke in favour of a public hall, gymnasium and reading room to be built in Abbey Fields, but Councillor Crouch cautioned that such a building could not be erected in the Abbey Fields under the conditions of purchase of the land. Instead, he proposed the restoration of the southern side of the ancient cloister garth of St Mary's Abbey to form a garden of peace, with a central memorial inscribed with the names of those who had died.

The proposal for a Cottage Hospital received warm support from Dr Asplen, who affirmed that a memorial should be of permanent benefit and real use, adding 'monuments are all very well if there is plenty of money to spend.'

This was questioned by Mr H. S. Powell, who noted the services available in neighbouring larger hospitals within reach of motor transport, and the chairman added that there were already six beds in Warneford Hospital in Leamington dedicated for the use of Kenilworth people. This was supported by a £4,000 trust fund that was unlikely to be transferable. His interpretation was endorsed by the Rev. Clements, a trustee of the hospital fund.

Mr Hacking questioned both the long-term cost of a hospital and any other project, such as the building of a library, which was more properly paid for by the rates. He supported Mr Crouch's idea for a cloister garden and seconded a proposal by Mr Crouch for the formation of a committee of thirty members to consider the possibilities and report back to another public meeting. After an interchange in which Mr C. W. Roberts counselled that the committee should not give preference to Mr Crouch's proposal for a cloister garden, it was agreed to elect a committee to consider all possibilities.

Thirty members were appointed under the chairmanship of Councillor Randall including a group representing discharged soldiers (Messrs Porter, Steen, Lees, Fulford and Walkley); relatives of the fallen (Messrs E. Reeves, A. H. Spicer, E. H. Jeacock, R. H. Clive and T. Mitchener), and other interests in the town (Dr Asplen, the Reverends W. Clements, J. W. Dennis, W. S. Scott, J. H. Denham, Mrs H. Quick, Mrs Herbert, Mrs Kevitt Rotherham, Mrs C. Randall, Lord Ernest Seymour, Lieut. Morton, and Messrs. C .W. Roberts, J. Farn, C. Randall, A. W. Street, T. Mason, G. Davies, A. H. Wamsley and W. Dencer). Mr Hadow was appointed secretary.

After this meeting, the local branch of the NatFedDDSS assembled to elect its officers These included Mr Porter (Chairman), Mr Lees (Treasurer), Mr Walkley (Secretary) and Mr Fulford (one of the eight members of the committee) who had just been elected to the Town Memorial Committee. The soldiers now had a corporate voice to put forward their own proposals.

At the first meeting of the War Memorial Committee, Mr Porter, on behalf of the NatFedDDSS, proposed that the War Memorial should consist of a public hall with a club room for the exclusive use of ex-service men. The cost was estimated at £3,000 to £4,000 and was supported by 11 votes in favour and 5 against. Mr Crouch's idea for a covered cloister, monument and garden was costed at £2,500 and received 11 votes in favour and 11 against.

Two other proposals received less support. Playing fields costing £2,000 to £3,000 received 4 votes for and 5 against; a free-standing monument on the Abbey Fields at the top of Abbey End costing £500 was the least favoured, with just 2 votes for and 12 against.

It was agreed to report back to a second public meeting on Saturday 25th June in the Drill Hall, to present all the proposals for a public vote.

At the public meeting, there was an over-whelming vote for a war memorial in the form of a public hall and a linked clubroom for discharged soldiers and sailors.

At this point, Mr Crouch requested that the other proposals be discussed and he gave a fuller explanation of his ideas for a 'garden of peace' in the Abbey Fields. There were others who gave it support, but when put to the vote, it was rejected by a large majority.

The idea for a monument at Abbey End was then considered. The Chairman, Mr Randall, announced that they already had the names of 112 fallen to place on it. However, Mr Hodges counselled that 'although nothing was too good for the brave fellows who had made it possible for us to live in this country' he feared that they would not be able to collect sufficient money for such a memorial.

It was then proposed by Mr Spicer (who had proposed it at the opening of the first town meeting) and seconded by Mr Porter, the chairman of the NatFedDDSS. It was lost by a large majority.

The fourth proposal—for a playing field—was reported by Mr Sholto Douglas to be under consideration by the council and was withdrawn.

A new War Memorial Committee of twenty members was elected to carry the proposal for a hall and clubroom forward; those elected were Messrs C. Randall, J. Crouch, C. W. Roberts, E. L. Andrews, R. Walker, Porter, E. P. Hodges, C. Barwell, H. S. Powell, W. H. Dencer, F. Harris, J. Lees, A. Hacking, Sholto Douglas, Wamsley, the Reverends J. W. Dennis, W. S. Scott and W. Clements, Mrs Randall and Mrs Rotherham.

On the following Saturday, the announcement of the decision in the *Warwick Advertiser and Leamington Gazette* was accompanied by a dissenting comment from a correspondent who observed that most of those who voted for the proposal were 'discharged soldiers and sailors' and 'the rest of the inhabitants are not greatly enamoured of the scheme.' While affirming 'nothing is too good for the men who have fought and conquered', the unnamed correspondent offered three arguments against the decision.

The first was the cost. The second was that there were already several good public halls including the Parochial Hall, the Drill Hall and the King's Arms Assembly Rooms, and that most former soldiers were already catered for by a range of organisations such as the Working Men's Club and the Conservative Club. The third was that 'in a few years' time, how many Kenilworth ex-service and servicemen will be here to take advantage of such a building?'

These concerns proved to be well-founded as the quest for a Town War Memorial changed course over the next eighteen months.

In the meantime, the committee addressed the organisation of Peace Day Celebrations which were to take place the next month.

Peace Day celebrations on 19th July

The Peace Treaty of Versailles between Germany and the Allied Powers was signed on 28 June 1919. For Kenilworth, this signalled the end of the war which, though usually called the '1914-1918 war', was to be commemorated on the Town Memorial from 1914 to 1919.

Saturday the 19th of July 1919 was declared a national holiday to celebrate the end of the war. After the success of the coronation celebrations for King George V, the day followed a similar pattern.

In the morning a 400-strong procession consisting of the returned soldiers and sailors accompanied by the Town Band marched from the Council House to the Abbey Fields for a united Service of Thanksgiving. A large floral cross was provided by Mrs Randall with a stand draped in purple, on which relatives and friends were able to place their wreaths and flowers. The choirs of St. Nicholas', St. John's and the Congregational Church were present.

After the service, Councillor Randall presented each man who had won distinction in the war with a token of the town's gratitude in the form of a certificate to be later exchanged for a gold albert chain. The

Mrs Randall plants the Peace Oak

full list as given in the *Kenilworth Advertiser* was as follows:

Presentations made earlier: The late Corporal Reeves DCM, The Late Staff-Sergeant Bricknell MM.

Presentations on the day: Brigadier-General Norman Herbert CMG DSO & Bar; Lieutenant Edwin C. Carter DSC; Sergeant Major Fisher MSM; Sergeant Charles Varney DCM; Sergeant Albert Mitchener DCM; Sergeant Arthur Drane MSM; Sergeant Askew MM; Sergeant H. L. Smith DCM; Lance-Corporal W. H. Hubbard Croix-de-Guerre; Signaller C. L. Grindrod MM; Rifleman L. Malin MM & Bar; Rifleman A. V. Hubbard MM; Private Ernest Salt MM & Bar; Corporal W. Aston MM & Bar; Private Tom Insall MM; Sergeant Major Finch DCM; Private Redmond DCM; Private C Wood DCM; Sergeant Hudson DCM; Quartermaster H. Satchwell, Belgian Croix-de-Guerre; W. Gilks MM.

Those not present: Captain J. R. Herbert, Croix-de-Guerre; Commander Godfrey Herbert DSO & Bar, Captain H. Stringer MBE; Captain C. F. L. Gibson MC; Commander A. G. Seymour DSO; Colonel C. Berkeley, CMG DSO OBE; Sergeant-Major W. Nixon, DCM; Sergeant George Adams MM.

The crowd, numbering several thousands, cheered heartily as each man was called for his award. Mrs Randall planted a peace oak tree and lunch was served to 400 guests, including returning service men.

In the afternoon, sports, games, entertainment and tea were arranged for the children. Mrs Randall provided each child with a commemorative mug and Mrs Salmon gave each child a medal. There were concerts in the Abbey Fields in the afternoon, and at the Parochial Hall and Abbey Hill Assembly Rooms in the evening, with a bonfire at Castle Hill to close the celebrations.

On the day it rained and the open-air sports and dancing were curtailed, but the rest of the activities proceeded with great success.

More Kenilworth soldiers die

In July and August, conditions in Kenilworth began to return to normal, with the resumption of the various shows connected with agriculture and horticulture. Reminders of the war, however, were never far away as three more Kenilworth solidiers died of their wounds.

Sergeant **Arthur Hazel** of New Row died in Northfield Sanatorium, Birmingham, in July. He had joined the 1st Royal Warwickshire Regiment early in 1915, and saw over two years' service in France. He was very severely wounded during the German offensive in the spring of 1918, being hit by shrapnel in the head. This caused an injury to the brain, which paralysed his right side. A bullet in his side penetrated and injured his lungs. He was also badly gassed.

Despite such a combination of injuries he made good progress. His head was successfully operated on, and his chest wound cleared up, but the deadly gas laid the foundation for the trouble from which he ultimately died. He spent his last 16 months in hospital, chiefly at Glasgow, Bramcote, Highfields (Birmingham), and later at Northfield. He was 29 years old and was buried in St Nicholas' Churchyard.

Private **Harry Ellis** of the Durham Light Infantry also died in July 1919 having been discharged because of illness in 1918.

Private **Frank Hewitt**—the son of Mr and Mrs Hewitt of Mill End, whose brother William Hewitt was killed in action in 1914—died in Hollymoor Hospital, Northfield, Birmingham on the 15th of August 1919. Frank had joined up three years before when he was 18, and had the misfortune to injure his foot in bayonet drill in April 1917. The injury took a bad turn, and developed into tuberculosis, necessitating amputation in March, 1918.

Frank was in hospital for nearly two years, initially on the Isle of Wight, and later in London.

Private Frank Hewitt

Finally, at the request of his parents, who felt the strain and expense of continually travelling such a distance, he was moved to Birmingham where he died. The funeral took place at the Parish Church on the afternoon of Thursday, August 18th but, at the request of the parents, the interment was performed without military honours. His headstone (pictured on page 24) also commemorates his brother William, whose body was never found.

The King's suggestion for the celebration of Armistice Day

At the suggestion of King George V, the first anniversary of Armistice day was to be marked by 'Two Minutes Silence' at the eleventh hour of the eleventh day of the eleventh month. On November 11th at 11.00 a.m., there was to be a calling to silence by the tolling of bells and wailing of sirens. Everyone, wherever they were, should stop their work or play for two minutes to 'direct their thoughts to the memory of those who died for us and by whose sacrifice we live.'

The first anniversary of the Armistice was celebrated in Kenilworth with great enthusiasm and devout thankfulness. The evening service at St Nicholas' was crowded with representatives of the various town organizations showing their respect. A very large number of ex-servicemen were present and the offertory was given to the Town War Memorial Fund.

The War Memorial project continues

The Kenilworth War Memorial Committee continued with its fund raising. Councillor Randall reported that the first donation of a gold sovereign had been made fittingly by a demobbed soldier but that only £5 had been collected in all. The minister of Abbey Hill Congregational Church, the Rev. W. S. Scott, gave a lecture in aid of the War Memorial and raised another £5.

The Committee estimated the cost for a public hall with club premises attached for the disabled and demobilised soldiers and sailors at £8,000. Following Armistice Day, a public appeal for funds was launched to carry out the scheme. Donations and promises were made for around £1,500, which fell far short of what was necessary.

At a meeting on December 6th, it was apparent that the agreed scheme could not be fulfilled. There now seemed to be a broad opinion opposed to a memorial in this form, although there was broad sympathy for

ALFRED AITKEN.	W.J. DRANE-OVERS.	HARRY MANTON.	CONSTANCE SEYMOUR.
SIDNEY C. AITKEN.	JAMES DREW.	C.J.W. MARTIN.	ALFRED SKELSEY.
ERNEST T. ASHMORE.	ALBERT E. DILWORTH.	HAROLD C. MARTIN.	JAMES SMITH.
BERTIE C. BANNARD.	WILLIAM E. EALES.	JAMES MARVIN.	WILLIAM J. SMITH.
WALTER J. BARBER.	OLIVER EDMOND.	CHARLES MATTHEWS.	ARTHUR SPICER.
EDWARD V. BARKER.	HARRY ELLIS.	W.H. McCOUSINS.	THOMAS STANLEY.
HENRY BARNETT.	DONALD EWEN.	GEORGE MITCHINER.	GEORGE SWANN.
HAROLD C. BATES.	FRANK E. FENERAN.	HARRY MITCHINER.	F.E. TAYLOR.
FREDERICK BAYLISS.	ERNEST FRAZIER.	JOHN C. MORGAN.	EDGAR THOMPSON.
WILLIAM BEAVERS.	GEORGE H. FRAZER.	CHARLES MOWBRAY.	JIM TOOKEY.
H.L. BIOMEAD.	VICTOR GARDNER.	JESSE MOWE.	REGINALD C. TWEEDY.
JOHN W. BRADSHAW.	JOHN GARRETT.	F.D. MULCAHY.	TREVOR TWEEDY.
GEORGE BRICKNELL.	ARTHUR GILKS.	CHARLES W. NEWEY.	EDGAR E. VINCENT.
H.G.R. BOYT.	ALBERT E. GILLAM.	ALFRED G. NIXON.	SPENCER WALTON.
HERBERT BUCKINGHAM.	W HENRY GRAINGER.	ALBERT E. OVERTON.	NORMAN J. WARD.
CHARLES S. BURTON.	ARTHUR E. GREEN.	W. JACOB PARKYN.	WILLIAM G. WARD.
SIDNEY BUTLER.	LEONARD GREEN.	FRED H. PITTAWAY.	HARVEY WARREN.
WALTER CANNON.	CHARLES H. GREGORY.	FRANCIS PLANT.	WILLIAM H. WATSON.
CHARLIE CARTER.	JAMES HARRIS.	JOSEPH PRATT.	FRANK WEBB.
CYRIL W. CARTER.	RICHARD HENRY HARRIS.	WALTER T. RAWLINGS.	WILLIAM WEBB.
JACK CASIMORE.	ARTHUR W. HAZEL.	CHARLES S. REED.	EDWARD J. WEBSTER.
ALBERT J. CAY.	WILLIAM HEWITT.	ALFRED REEVE.	ROBERT G. WEBSTER.
WILLIAM CHALONER.	WILLIAM HICKMAN.	EDWARD REEVE.	EDWARD WHATELEY.
HAROLD CLIFT.	HARRY HINCKS.	LEONARD REEVE.	TOM WHATELEY.
REGINALD D. CLIVE.	ERNEST H. HOPKINS.	HARRY REYNOLDS.	DUDLEY WHITE.
REGINALD J. COLLETT.	CHRISTOPHER HORSLEY.	JAMES REYNOLDS.	FRED WILKSHIRE.
ROBERT COLMAN.	ARTHUR J. HUBBARD.	CARLTON RIVERS.	WILLIAM WILKSHIRE.
GEORGE COLOMB.	SAM INSALL.	WILLIAM ROBERTSON.	SACHEVEREL D. WILMOT.
MERVYN COLOMB.	WILLIAM A. JAKEMAN.	HAROLD RUDDOCK.	OSWALD WINSTANLEY.
HARRY COX.	GUY E. KIDD.	ARTHUR SADLER.	FRANK HEWITT.
WILFRED G. DANIELL.	GILBERT LIGGINS.	ARTHUR SAWYER.	AUSTIN MARTIN.
VICTOR DRANE.	ERNEST LETTS.	LAURIE SEEKINGS.	FRANK SABIN.

The St Nicholas' War Memorial Tablet

some kind of scheme that benefitted both the members who returned and the dependants of the honoured dead. The committee decided to ask the Kenilworth Branch of the NatFedDDSS to submit alternative schemes to be presented to another public meeting in the town.

1920

At the next meeting of the War Memorial Committee on the 5th January in the new year, the ex-servicemen re-iterated their wish to have their own club. It was now fully apparent that there were insufficient funds to carry out the original proposal. By a vote of 6 to 2, the committee proposed a memorial in the form of a cenotaph. This proposition was put to a further public meeting on Thursday, January 22nd where the final decision was taken to place a cenotaph at the top of Abbey End, facing the road. The ex-servicemen did not oppose the decision, but continued to express the need for a club of their own which would raise funds in support of the dependents of those who had fallen.

Meanwhile, the plaques for the churches of St Nicholas and St John were proceeding satisfactorily and were ready to be unveiled.

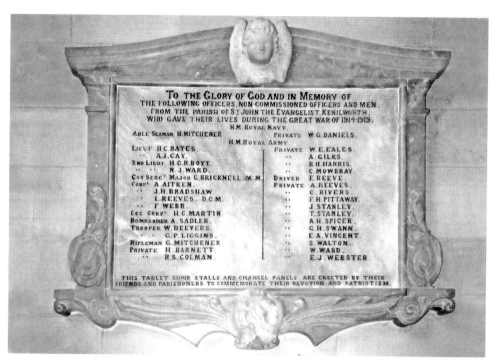

The St John War Memorial Tablet

The Memorial Tablets in the churches of St Nicholas and St John

The St Nicholas' Memorial was dedicated by the Vicar in February and attended by a procession of a hundred members of the NatFedDDSS. The collection totalled £18 and was given to the ex-servicemen's benevolent fund. The church magazine reported:

> *The Dedication of the War Memorial Tablet took place in the Parish church on Sunday afternoon February 1st at 3.15. The ceremony was performed by the Vicar in the presence of about 800 people, representing all sections of the community. There are about 120 names inscribed on the Tablet of the men of Kenilworth who gave their lives for their King and Country in the Great War. It is a beautiful Memorial, and is worthy of its great purpose. Special seats were reserved near the monument for the relatives of the heroic dead. May they rest in the Peace of God.*

The memorial in St John's Church was dedicated in March by the Bishop of Coventry.

The two memorials serve different purposes and the names common to both differ in small details. The St Nicholas' Memorial was intended to include all those who died from the town and has 128 names. These are broadly in alphabetical order, except for three late additions: Frank Hewitt who died in late 1919, Austin Martin who died shortly after the dedication of the memorial, and Frank Sabin. Frank was one of several soldiers whose name was only added to the memorials at a later date. He was a Private in the 2nd Battalion Royal Warwickshire Regiment and died on the 25th September 1915; his next of kin was recorded as his father, who lived not in Kenilworth, but in Gloucester.

Thirty-one of the thirty-two names on the St John's Memorial are included on the St Nicholas' tablet. The exception is Private John Stanley, whose parents lived in Bulkington Cottages, Kenilworth. His brother James Thomas Stanley appears on both memorials.

Others omitted from the St Nicholas' tablet include Charles Butler, Arthur Lake and Cuthbert Allen. Charles Butler was a Catholic, and was not on the St Nicholas' list, (although another Catholic, William Watson, appears on the memorial tablet). Arthur Lake's next of kin, his sister, now lived in Coventry and Cuthbert Allen's father, the Rev. Allen, who was minister of the Congregational Church during the war had subsequently moved to South Yardley in Birmingham.

Competition for the Design of the War Memorial

On February 5th, 1920, the War Memorial Committee voted to open the design of a War Memorial to public competition, with prizes of £50 and £25 for the best two designs selected by the President of the Birmingham Architectural Association. An upper limit of £900 was set on the cost, with the whole town to be kept informed of progress.

By late April, twenty-five designs had been submitted and were placed on show in the Council House in mid-May. There was general agreement that the best design was by the sculptor F. W. Doyle-Jones from Chelsea, estimated at a cost of between £900 and £1000.

As the summer progressed, other details were agreed and the land at the top of Abbey End, by the entrance to Abbey Fields, was donated by Kenilworth Urban District Council.

In April and May, two more organisations in Kenilworth paid their tributes to their own war dead. In April, the members of the Loyal Caledonian Corks Lodge of Oddfellows held a dinner to honour their ex-service brothers. Fifty out of 221 members of the lodge had joined the forces. Five fell in action: J. Tookey, L. Green, J. Garner, H. Reynolds, and A. Dilworth. All but J. Garner are commemorated on the Town Memorial.

In May, seventy members of the local lodge of the Druids met at the Virgin's Inn (now the Virgins and Castle) to unveil a carved oak memorial to honour the brothers who had died. Those named were Harry Hincks, A. Sadler, R. C. Tweedy, C. Strange and J. Moore. The first three are also commemorated on the Town Memorial.

The Ex-Servicemen seek their own clubhouse

The NatFedDDSS had grown to 833 members and continued to pursue its plans for a clubhouse as its own memorial to the war. The original grand plan costing around £8000 was out of the question and they began to think in terms of more modest accommodation. The cost of living was now more than double pre-war levels and there were serious difficulties in making earnings stretch to cover personal needs. Nationally there were strikes in engineering companies and by steelworkers, while coalworkers were on short-time. An item in *The Kenilworth Advertiser* reflected the national predicament:

> *In common with the rest of the country, Kenilworth is feeling the slump in trade. Locally there is not a great deal of employment outside agriculture, the tannery, brickworks and skin works. The Tannery is the biggest employer.*

In the shadow of increasing hardship, an appeal by the President of the NatFedDDSS for support in April initially raised only £66 18s 1d. A second plea brought another £61 including £50 from Mr and Mrs Kevitt Rotherham. The day was saved by Councillor Randall who made a personal contribution of £500, together with a promise of additional funding from the national United Services Fund which stood at over one and a half million pounds for the country as a whole.

Thoughts turned to the possibility of using ex-army buildings at an estimated cost of £2500 for an army hut and a piece of land, of which the main cost was for the land. Again Mr Randall came to the rescue, offering a piece of land in School Lane for a modest rent that could be paid out of annual subscriptions.

War Memorial Appeal

In the autumn of 1920, the final details of the War Memorial were agreed at a cost of around £1,000 and 1,500 letters were sent out in November seeking support for the War Memorial. The carefully worded letter encouraged every resident to contribute something so that all could share in a lasting tribute to the fallen. It encouraged those who had promised support for the earlier scheme to give at least a proportion of the original subscription to the memorial project.

The response was extremely disappointing. Subscriptions received were only £357 18s 6d. Of this total, £100 came from Mr Randall himself with three other donations of £50. Around 100 replies were received in all with smaller sums making up the total. Fourteen hundred people asked to contribute by written letter failed even to reply.

Meanwhile, thanks to the benevolence of Mr Randall, progress was being made on the new facilities for the NatFedDDSS in School Lane. Two wooden buildings had been acquired from the Government. One, which had been used as an army chapel, would be the club premises and an ordinary army hut would be adapted to house the steward.

Kenilworth War Memorial Committee.

Chairman : Mr. C. RANDALL, C.C., "Abbotsfield," Kenilworth.
Treasurer : Mr. H. S. POWELL, L.C. & Mid. Bank, Kenilworth.
Hon. Sec. : Mr. F. PIDGEON, 7 Stoneleigh Road, Kenilworth.

September, 1920.

DEAR SIR OR MADAM,

The Committee appointed by the Town to carry through the provision of a War Memorial, have selected a design which has been exhibited in the window of the Council House for a month and has met with general approval. It is the desire of the Committee that every resident in the Town should be given an opportunity of expressing appreciation of the sacrifice made on their behalf by those who laid down their lives that England might live. The total cost of the Memorial will be about £1,000, and the Committee wish to put the work in hand as soon as possible. It is, therefore, respectfully urged that Donations should be sent to—

MR. C. RANDALL, *Chairman ;*
MR. H. S. POWELL, *Treasurer ;* or
MR. F. PIDGEON, *Hon. Secretary.*

The Committee hope that every resident will contribute something, so that all may share in raising a lasting tribute to the brave men of Kenilworth who gave their lives for their country.

If you have already promised a Donation to the original scheme, which included the provision of a Public Hall, but which has since been found to be impracticable, may we ask that your offer—or a proportion thereof—be extended to the present scheme, to enable the Town to erect a Memorial that will for all time prove that Kenilworth was not ungrateful to those who maintained, at the cost of their lives, her credit in the Great War.

We are, yours faithfully,

CHARLES RANDALL.
H. S. POWELL.
F. PIDGEON.

THE KENILWORTH WAR MEMORIAL is to be an obelisk of Portland stone, square in plan, upon three steps, and will be erected as a roadside monument, slightly set back from the pathway, at the selected site at the top of Abbey End, Kenilworth.

The front upper panel will contain a dedication, and the lower panel an inscription, the three remaining panels being left for the names of those who gave their lives. The only decoration will be a carved lion's head on the upper part of the column holding a wreath of laurel.

The total height, with steps, is to be 20ft. 6in.

Robertson & Sons, Printers, Three Spires Press, Greyfriars Lane, Coventry.

The Letter of Appeal and the Design for the War Memorial

Other new facilities opened during the year included a library of 500 books at the Council House, funded by the Carnegie Trustees, and a new picture house to show films in Station Road. The town also celebrated the announcement that Mr Albert Cay and Mrs Quick had both been awarded the Order of the British Empire, he as treasurer and she as secretary of the Local War Pension Committee.

Further soldiers' deaths

During 1920, two more soldiers died of injuries sustained in the war. **Austin Martin** had been severely wounded in action in 1914, and had lived a restricted life back in Kenilworth with one arm badly damaged and virtually useless. He was admitted to hospital in May 1919 and had eight or nine operations on the arm before it finally turned septic and he died. He was given a military funeral in St Nicholas' Church on Sunday June 20th and buried in Kenilworth Cemetery.

Leonard Norman Parkyn also died after a long period of suffering. He had been wounded in action in March 1918 and taken prisoner. On his release in January 1919, he was transferred to hospital in Scotland, returning to Kenilworth in July 1919, and dying at home over a year later on August 30th 1920.

1921

In the new year, the Vicar of St Nicholas made an appeal in the parish magazine for financial support to pay for the costs incurred in preserving the abbey ruins, which were now closed for burials. Finances were also tight at St John's where the vicar declared, 'we must work hard and spend less.'

On New Years Day, three hundred ex-service men's children were entertained at the new picture house in Station Road, and paraded back to the newly-opened club premises in School Lane for tea, leaving for home at 6.00 p.m. with a penny and an orange.

An Unemployment Relief Committee was appointed to deal with the distress in Kenilworth caused by shortage of work. A house-to-house collection was made in March, raising £28 0s 9d for the unemployed.

The disappointing response to the War Memorial Appeal resulted in the decision to modify the design for an all-in cost of £600. This would be accomplished by the designer reducing the height from sixteen blocks to twelve. He had been successful elsewhere in tendering for the building of memorials, including one at Weymouth which was to occupy his time before he completed the memorial in Kenilworth.

Nationally a proposal was made to unite the ex-servicemen's organisations throughout the country and the British Legion Committee was formed to consolidate a national organisation founded on brotherhood and friendship.

By the end of April, coal stocks were nearly exhausted because of the national coal strike. Unemployment was rife in Kenilworth and increased with the closure of two brickyards due to lack of coal.

Labour Day was very subdued. A procession arranged for various organisations and kindred societies totalled less than twenty people. It headed past the Working Men's Club, Abbey Hill, Albion Street and School Lane to a service at the Parish Church.

In June it was reported that demobilisation of the Army Reserve was to begin at once. The Prime Minister appealed to employers of labour to re-instate reservists in their former employment. The national coal strike finally ended in July.

The Memorial in the Working Men's Club

In August, the Working Men's Club unveiled a Memorial in the hall of their club inscribed with all the names of club members who served in the war. In the centre were those who lost their lives: G. Bricknell, J. Moore, E. Ashmore, H. J. Reynolds and L. Green. Four of these were commemorated on the St Nicholas' Memorial and would appear on the Town Memorial the next year. However, J. Moore—who had also been honoured as a member of the local Druids—does not appear on either and we have been unable to trace any further details.

The Memorial in the Kenilworth Working Men's Club

By this time, the interest in the Working Men's Club Band had waned and it followed the path of many other bands in Kenilworth into oblivion.

At the end of September a drumhead memorial service organised by the local branch of the British Legion was held in the Abbey Fields and attended by over 1,500. The procession included the Fire Brigade, Police, Druids, Railwaymen, Guides and Friendly Societies. Rev. Swallow from Coventry, who had been an army chaplain and represented the service men of Kenilworth on such occasions, referred to the treatment of ex-soldiers: 'Men at Coventry were lining up to collect bread and margarine which was all a country could give them.'

By October, eight men were put to work on stone-breaking for the Kenilworth Council as relief work for the unemployed. It was decided to hire another steam roller for repairs to roads, thus giving employment to two gangs. At a council meeting, a suggestion for excavation of the ruins in the Abbey Fields, using unemployed men, met with approval. At the end of the month about 100 were receiving out-of-work relief.

Albert Cay, the former High Sherriff of Warwickshire, died in November having received his OBE. Albert moved to Kenilworth in 1891 to live in the grand house at Woodside and to run his business as owner of the glass works of Messrs. James Stevens & Co. in Birmingham. He was a considerable benefactor to the town and to St John's Church. He was buried in Ashow, with the Bishop of Coventry officiating.

The Methodist Memorial

In November, Armistice Day was observed once more with a two minute silence. All the church services were well attended.

On the 17th of November, the Wesleyan Methodist Church dedicated its own memorial which consisted of new Sunday School rooms and a tablet to those members of the church who fell in the war. The tablet was unveiled by Colonel Fiddian Green and listed the names of W. Hickman, A. Sawyer, E. Frazer, E. Vincent, C. Mowbray, J. Pratt, J. Mowe, F. Sabin and R. Harris.

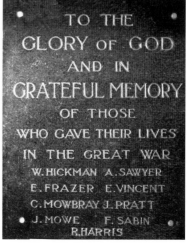

The Methodist Memorial Tablet

1922

The new year began with an influenza epidemic in the town. There was seasonal snowfall and the steep slopes in Abbey Fields were filled with people enjoying the thrill of a down-hill toboggan run.

On Saturdays, members of Kenilworth British Legion opened a market selling meat and vegetables at reasonable prices in one of their two buildings. It proved to be highly successful in a community with 233 men unemployed and a further seasonal layoff of agricultural workers and gardeners bringing the number to around 300.

The Dedication of the War Memorial

At the beginning of February the Memorial was erected on the site in Abbey Hill, constructed from twelve blocks of Portland stone. The front panel contained a dedication and an inscription 'In grateful memory of those from Kenilworth who gave their lives in the Great War 1914-1919. Lest we forget.' The side panels were inscribed with the names of those who died in the war.

The unveiling of the War Memorial took place on Sunday, February 26th, 1922 in pouring rain. The report in *The Kenilworth Advertiser* remarked on the poignancy of the occasion:

The Crowds await the unveiling of the War Memorial in the pouring rain

The unveiling of Kenilworth's War Memorial took place on Sunday afternoon last, in the presence of from 2,000 to 3,000 of the inhabitants, who braved the elements to do homage to the memory of those whose names were engraved on the Memorial. Rain was falling when from two o'clock the people wended their way to Abbey Hill, the site of the Memorial, or to the Council House, where at 2.45 the procession started.

The order of the procession, in which about 400 marched, was as follows: Inspector Hawkes, the band of the 7th Batt. Royal Warwickshire Regiment; Mr Charles Randall (chairman of the Memorial Committee); Lord Leigh; and Mr J. E. Jackson (chairman of the Council), walking abreast, and followed by members of the Council and officers; members of the Memorial Committee; the Kenilworth Volunteer Fire Brigade (under the command of Capt. Dr. W. Asplen); members of the British Legion; the local section (ladies) of the British Red Cross Society; the Girl Guides; the Druids; the Loyal Elizabethan and Loyal Dudley Lodges of Oddfellows; the Buffs and other Friendly Societies; the Working Men's and Conservative Clubs, the Post Office Officials; and the Railwaymen. Mr Parkin was marshall.

Headed by the band the procession moved off promptly to time, but the crowd was so dense at the site that more than half of those

The Unveiling with Mr Randall on the left and the Clergy and Lord Leigh to the right

participating in the march were unable to hear the prayers and speeches made in the course of the ceremony. Rain was falling heavily, and the scene was just a mass of umbrellas, upon which the rain caused such a noise that only those in the immediate vicinity of the speakers could hear their words. Seats within the enclosure had been reserved for the relatives of the fallen: and Messrs. Wilkshire, Reeves, Frazer, and Green, each of whom had lost two sons in the war, were in attendance to assist at the unveiling.

THE CEREMONY

Led by the band the crowd sang the hymn, 'O God our help in ages past' and the Rev. W. Stuart Scott then offered a beautifully worded prayer.

Mr C. Randall asked Lord Leigh to unveil the Memorial, which his Lordship proceeded to do. He paid a touching tribute to the memory of the departed, who, he said, had died that those present might live in a free land. Let them always remember those who had died, and so order their own lives to be worthy of the sacrifices made for them.

The dedication was performed by the Vicar of Kenilworth (the Rev. J. W. Dennis), and the 'Last Post' and the 'Reveille' were sounded by the buglers of the 7th Batt. R.W.R. The Hymn was sung, 'On the Resurrection Morning.'

The Rev. Kenelm Swallow, M.C., B.A. said that that column, with its list of 132 names, would be intolerable did it merely signify that men had died, with its constant reminder of the past, but like as was the death of Jesus Christ, it was rather a monument of life and victory. Like the Cross, that Memorial was a beacon to remind them of the one certain hope when father, brother, sister, mother, meet again. It was a symbol of everlasting glory and renown. God is alone the Comforter of the mourners for in Him there is no death. It was well that it was pouring with rain—he hoped that it might pour at all unveiling ceremonies so that they might recall that those who endured the years in the trenches were drenched with water and blood, days and nights on end. Those who, for reasons of comfort, were not there to pay tribute should bear that in mind, and those who had wealth and failed to respond to the appeal should also think. He hoped that the fair-weather patriots sitting at home in comfort would realise that these men died to save those homes.

In Grateful Memory of those from Kenilworth who Gave their Lives :: in the Great War, 1914 = 1919. ::

"LEST WE FORGET."

Aitken, A.	Drane-Overs, W. J.	Letts, E.	Seekings, L.
Aitken, S. C.	Drew, J.	Manton, H.	Sabin, F.
Ashmore, E. T.	Dilworth, A. E.	Martin, A.	Seymour, C. (Miss)
Bannard, B. C.	Eales, W. E.	Martin, C. J. W.	Skelsey, A.
Barker, E.	Edmond, O.	Martin, H. C.	Smith, J.
Barber, W. J.	Ellis, H.	Marvin, J.	Smith, W. J.
Barnett, H.	Ewen, D.	Matthews, C.	Spicer, A. H.
Bates, H. C.	Faxon, H.	McCousins, W. H.	Stanley, T.
Bayliss, F.	Feneran, F. E.	Mitchiner, G.	Swann, G.
Beavers, W.	Frazer, E.	Mitchiner, H.	Taylor, F. E.
Bidmead, H. L.	Frazer, G. H.	Morgan, J. C.	Thompson, E.
Bradshaw, J. W.	Gardner, V.	Mowbray, C.	Tookey, J.
Bricknell, G.	Garrett, J.	Mowe, J.	Tweedy, R. C.
Boyt, H. G. R.	Gilks, A.	Mulcahy, F. D.	Tweedy, T.
Buckingham, H.	Gillam, A. E.	Newey, C. W.	Vincent, E.
Buckingham, A. E.	Grainger, W. H.	Nixon, A. G.	Walton, S.
Burton, C. S.	Green, A. E.	Overton, A. E.	Ward, N. J.
Butler, S.	Green, L.	Parkyn, W. J.	Ward, W. G.
Cannon, W.	Gregory, C. H.	Pettaway, F. H.	Warren, H.
Carter, C.	Harris, J.	Plant, F.	Watson, W. H.
Carter, C. W.	Harris, R. H.	Pratt, J.	Webb, F.
Cashmore, J.	Hazel, A. W.	Rawlins, W. T.	Webb, W.
Cay, A. J.	Hewitt, F.	Reed, C. S.	Webster, E. J.
Chaloner, W.	Hewitt, W.	Reeve, A.	Webster, R. G.
Clift, H.	Hickman, W.	Reeve, E.	Whateley, E.
Clive, R. D.	Hincks, H.	Reeve, L.	Whateley, T.
Collett, R. J.	Hopkins, E. H.	Reynolds, H.	White, D.
Colman, R.	Horsley, C.	Reynolds, J.	Wilkshire, F.
Colomb, G.	Hubbard, A. J.	Rivers, C.	Wilkshire, W.
Colomb, M.	Insall, S.	Robertson, W.	Wilmot, S. D.
Cox, H.	Jakeman, W. A.	Ruddock, H.	Winstanley, O.
Daniell, W. G.	Kidd, G. E.	Sadler, A.	
Drane, V.	Liggins, G.	Sawyer, A.	——

The List of Soldiers on the War Memorial as given on the Programme

Mr Randall, in thanking Lord Leigh and the others who had attended to take part in the ceremony, referred to the men to whom the Memorial had been erected—those men who had made the supreme sacrifice, and were now with the Great Redeemer in Peace awaiting those who are near and dear to them. He then asked Councillor Jackson to accept on behalf of the Council the custody of the Memorial.

Councillor Jackson, in undertaking the duty, said that it would be a sacred care to keep evergreen the memory of those men.

The Rev. W. Clements prayed that, remembering the devotion of the glorious dead, they all might live in union and peace, comforting those who mourn.

Very many floral tributes were then laid at the foot of the Memorial by the relatives of the fallen and on behalf of many public bodies. The National Anthem was sung and the ceremony concluded.

A collection was taken for the distress fund for the unemployed.

A large crowd still remained, unaffected by the downpour and discomfort of the day, and these only gradually dispersed.

Although the Rev. Swallow is reported to have said there were 132 names, the programme for the unveiling lists 130. These are the 128 names in the Parish Church plus A. E. Buckingham and H. R. Faxon.

Private **Albert Edward Buckingham** is recorded on the published list of 'Soldiers who died in the war' as living in Kenilworth and enlisting in the Royal Warwickshire 10th Battalion at Coventry. He was reported missing on 25th of September 1918 and later presumed killed. His widow lived at Sparkhill, Birmingham.

Herbert Faxon was the son of Mr Richard and Mrs Eva Marion Faxon of School Lane. He was a driver with the 76th Battery, Royal Field Artillery and died in hospital in Mesopotamia on 30th August, 1916. He was buried in Baghdad.

The various memorials differ in minor details. For instance, W. T. Rawlings on the St Nicholas' Memorial is given as W. T. Rawlins on the Town Memorial. Other names which agree on these memorials differ on the St John's memorial, for instance, W. G. Daniell becomes W. G. Daniels, the brothers described earlier as Mitchener are recorded as Michiner in St Nicholas' and on the town Memorial, but become Michner in St John's. At the same time, the surname of Alfred and Leonard Reeve becomes Reeves in St John's.

Changes on the Memorial after the dedication

In later years, nine other names from the Great War were added to the Town Memorial. Two were soldiers who died after the Memorial was completed:

Harry Stanley of High Street died in hospital in 1923;

Wilfred George Cox, the brother of Harry Cox, died on 31st December 1923.

Seven others who had already died when the Memorial was unveiled were omitted initially but were added at a later date. These are:

Charles Austin Butler, a Catholic, omitted from the St Nicholas' plaque;

Arthur Lake, whose next of kin was given as his sister in Coventry following the death of his Kenilworth parents;

Cuthbert Allen, who had lived in South Africa before the war and was the son of the minister of the Congregational Church who subsequently moved to Birmingham;

John Stanley, brother of James Stanley, whose parents lived at Bulkington Cottages just outside Kenilworth;

Leonard Norman Parkyn, the brother of William Jacob Parkyn, who died at home in Pleasaunce Farm Cottages, Kenilworth in 1920;

John W. Weyman, husband of Margaret Weyman of 7 Hammond's Terrace, Clinton Lane, Kenilworth, who joined the Royal Welsh Fusiliers and whose family home was in Wales;

William James West, died in Hatton Asylum on the 2nd November 1917, and his link with Kenilworth is currently unknown.

Two names have occurred in our narrative who seem to have Kenilworth connections but are not recorded on the Town Memorial.

Alfred Miles is mentioned in the Parish Church Magazine Roll of Honour 1918, but not subsequently.

J. Moore is on the memorials of the Working Men's Club and the Druids.

In addition, there are names that were added in the final pages of the St Nicholas' Church Roll of Honour, which was on public display in the nave of the church for many years. These include:

George Baterbee, wounded three times in 1916, discharged as unfit for service, died in Kenilworth 21st February 1924;

Ernest Martin, stationed at Kenilworth Police Station before the war, served in the war, demobbed in 1919, died in Kenilworth, 28th July 1924;

William Dyde, served in the RAF in France, 1915–1919, died 1932.

Edward Griffiths, died 2nd March 1914, a native of Birmingham, brother of Mrs L. Webb of Whitemoor, Kenilworth;

George John Hudson (no further information);

George Frederic Reeve, died 1929;

George Steward, died 1930;

James Hewitt (no further information).

The search for a definitive list of those from Kenilworth who died is no simple matter. In his speech at the end of the war, the Chairman of the Council, Mr Randall, mentioned that 90 Kenilworth men had died out of 836 who had joined up, based on the list compiled by Mr Hadow from the National Registry of Notification of Enlistments. The collaboration between Mr Hadow and St Nicholas' Church, with information collected via the local press, produced 125 names for the dedication of the St Nicholas' memorial tablet, with three later additions bringing it to the 128 names that appear today. Two more were added to this list to give 130 on the Town War Memorial on the day of its unveiling, with nine more added later to give the current total of 139 who fell in, or died as a result of, the Great War.

Following the Second World War, in 1951 bronze plaques were cast and placed on the front and two side panels of the War Memorial covering the original inscriptions that had been carved directly onto the stone. These plaques incorporated the original dedication and inscription, and the names of those who died in the First World War. A fourth bronze plaque was placed on the rear of the Memorial with the names of 68 men and women from Kenilworth who died in World War II.

A later addition is the name of one man killed in Korea in 1952.

The original left-hand side of the Memorial   *... enlarged to show the original names*

LETTS. E.	SAWYER A.
LIGGINS. G.	SEYMOUR.CONSTANCE
MANTON. H.	SEEKINGS. L.
MARTIN A.	SKELSEY A.
MARTIN C.W.J.	SMITH J.
MARTIN. H.C.	SMITH. W.J.
MARVIN. J.	SPICER. A.H.
MATTHEWS. C.	STANLEY H.
McCOUSINS W.H.	STANLEY. J
MITCHINER G.	STANLEY J T
MITCHINER. H.	SWANN. G.
MORGAN J. C	TAYLOR. F.E.
MOWBRAY. C	THOMPSON E
MOWE. J.	TOOKEY J.
MULCAHY. F.D	TWEEDY R.C.
NEWEY C.W.	TWEEDY. T.
NIXON. A.G.	VINCENT E.A.
OVERTON.A.E.	WALTON .S
PARKYN. L.N.	WARD. N.J.
PARKYN. W.J.	WARD W.G.
PITTAWAY F. H.	WARREN. H.
PLANT. F.	WATSON. W.H
PRATT. J.	WEBB. F.
RAWLINS.W.T.	WEBB W.
REED. C.S.	WEBSTER E. J.
REEVE. A.	WEBSTER.R.G.
REEVE. E.	WEST. W.J.
REEVE. H.L.	WEYMAN .J.W.
REYNOLDS. H.	WHATELEY. E.
REYNOLDS. J.	WHATELEY. T.
RIVERS. C.	WHITE. D.
ROBERTSON. W.	WILKSHIRE. F.
RUDDOCK. H.	WILKSHIRE. W
SABIN. F.	WILMOT. S.D.
SADLER. A.	WINSTANLEY. O.

IN GRATEFUL
MEMORY OF
THOSE FROM
KENILWORTH
WHO GAVE
THEIR LIVES
IN THE
GREAT WAR
1914-1919

LEST WE FORGET

AITKEN A	DILWORTH A.E.
AITKEN. S.C.	DRANE. V
ALLEN. G.C.L.	DRANE-OVERS W.J.
ASHMORE. E.T.	DREW J.
BANNARD. B.C.	EALES W. E.
BARBER. W.J.	EDMOND O
BARKER E.	ELLIS H.
BARNETT. H.	EWEN D.
BATES H.C.	FAXON H.
BAYLISS. F.	FENEREN F.E.
BEEVERS W	FRAZER E A
BIDMEAD H.L.	FRAZER G.H
BOYT H G R.	GARDNER.H.V
BRADSHAW J.W	GARRETT J.
BRICKNELL G	GILKS A
BUCKINGHAM A.E.	GILLAM A.E.
BUCKINGHAM H.	GRAINGER W.H.
BURTON C.S.	GREEN A.E.
BUTLER C.A.	GREEN H.L.
BUTLER. S	GREGORY C.H.
CANNON W	HARRIS J
CARTER C.	HARRIS R.H.
CARTER C.W.	HAZEL A.W.
CASHMORE J	HEWITT F.
CAY. A.J.	HEWITT H.W
CHALONER W	HICKMAN W
CLIFFT. H.	HINCKS H.
CLIVE R.D.	HOPKINS E.H.
COLLETT. R.J.	HORSLEY C.
COLMAN. R.	HUBBARD A.J.
COLOMB G.	INSALL S.
COLOMB. M.	JAKEMAN W.A.
COX H.	KIDD G.E.
COX. W.G.	LAKE A.
DANIELL W.G.	

THESE GAVE THEIR LIVES IN THE WAR OF 1939-1945	
ASHFIELD. L.C.	HUGGINS. J.
BANHAM. G.	JARRETT. G.W.J.
BARNSLEY. A.E.	KETTLE. A.P.
BENTLEY. H.	LAMLEY. A.J.
BENTLEY. L.	LAMB. B.
BLENCOWE R.W.	LATHAM. C.L.
BONEHAM. A.	LITTLEJOHN. R.
BOUSTOULLER L	MATTHEWS C.E.W.
BREWER. D.H.	MORGAN. G.
BURT. R.	ODELL. A.
CARDWELL-HILL. L	POTTS. T.W.
CAREY-HILL. A.	POTTS. E.
CASTLE. C.H.	REDLEY. R.F.
CASTLE. R.	REED. N.A.
CLARKE. F.H.	SABIN. L.H.
COLLETT. L. E.	SAUL. J.
CONSTABLE. R. A.	SEWELL. R.E.
COOKE. O.J.	SHEEPY. V.C.
COX. C.S.	SHERWIN. J. E.
DAVIES. J.	STEELEY. H. J.
DAVIES. R.E.	STOCK. F. S.
DEAN. A.	TEALE. F. W.
DRURY. W. H.	THOMPSON. R.E
DUNN. A. E.	TOMPSON. G.
FLYNN. J.T.P.S.	WALTON. A. J.
FLYNN. W.T.S.	WALTON. D. H.
FLYNN. A.T.S	WEYMANN. J. E.
FOSTER K	WEBB. G.
GARRETT. L. R.	WHEATLEY. O. F.
GOLBY. C.	WILKINSON. P. L.
HALL. A. N.	WILKINSON. C. D.
HALL. R. H.	WILSON. S.
HAYES. R.G.	WORRALL. N. J.
HIBBERT. N.P.	WRIGHTON. T. J.W.

KOREA 1952

MUSGRAVE. R. F.

The plaques added to the War Memorial in 1951 and 1952
(left, front, right, back)

Afterword

The Kenilworth War Memorial carries upon it the names of 138 men and one woman who died in the Great War. The final difficulties in raising the funds to build a suitable memorial should not cloud our images of those days in the early twentieth century when the world was at war, nor of the times that followed when life was chastened by shortages and unemployment. Other towns and villages experienced similar difficulties and went through a similar sequence of struggle to properly honour those who had died.

In the new millenium, Kenilworth is a thriving community of nearly thirty thousand souls, five times the size of the smaller community whose spirit survived the privations of the First World War. Proudly at the top of the main shopping thoroughfare stands the town's memorial to those who fell in the defence of our freedom.

> *They shall grow not old as we that are left grow old,*
> *Age shall not weary them, nor the years condemn,*
> *At the going down of the sun, and in the morning,*
> *We will remember them.*

Appendix I: The Fallen in the Great War, Commemorated on the Kenilworth War Memorial

All the following are on today's town war memorial. The symbol * denotes names on the memorial on the day it was unveiled, + denotes those added later. Other letters note those commemorated in other ways: N St Nicholas' Memorial, J St John's, M Methodist, W Working Men's Club, P Post Office, D Druids, O Oddfellows.

AITKEN, Alfred *NJ

Corporal 17511, Oxford and Bucks Light Infantry.
Died at Bristol Southern Hospital, 26th April 1917,
three months after being wounded in France, aged 26.
Buried in Kenilworth Cemetery. Son of Mr and Mrs
Joseph Aitken of 16 White's Row, Kenilworth.

AITKEN, Sidney Charles *N

Private 10447, 2nd Battalion, Coldstream Guards.
Killed in action, 23rd October 1914, aged 19.
No known grave. Commemorated on the Ypres (Menin Gate) Memorial, Belgium.
Panel 11. Son of Mr William Charles and Mrs Harriett Elizabeth Aitken of 72
Clinton Lane, Kenilworth.

ALLEN, Cuthbert George Llewellin +

Second Lieutenant, 175th Field Company, Royal
Engineers.
Died of wounds in France, 3rd November 1915, aged 32.
Buried in Lijssenthoek Military Cemetery, Poperinge,
West-Vlaanderen, Belgium. II. A. I.
Son of Rev. Charles Llewellin and Mrs Blanche Lewis
Allen, of Waverley Road, Kenilworth.

ASHMORE, Ernest Thomas *NW

Stoker 1st Class, 301367, H.M. Submarine H5, Royal Navy.
Drowned in the Irish Sea, 2nd March 1918, aged 36.
Commemorated on the Portsmouth Naval Memorial.
Son of Mr Thomas and Mrs Elizabeth Ashmore of 5
Humphris St, Emscote,Warwick.
Husband of Lucy Sarah Ashmore of 50 Spring Lane,
Kenilworth.

BANNARD, Bertie Charles *[N]

Lance Sergeant 265857, 1st/7th Battalion, Royal
Warwickshire Regiment. Killed in action near
Ypres, 13th August, 1917, aged 27. No known grave.
Commemorated on the Ypres (Menin Gate) Memorial,
Belgium. Panel 8.
Son of the late Mr William and Mrs Sarah Bannard of
Albion St, Kenilworth.
Brother of Mr E. G. Bannard of 6 Little Virginia,
Kenilworth.

BARBER, Walter John *[NJ]

Private 1980, 2nd/7th Battalion, Royal Warwickshire
Regiment. Killed by a shell whilst helping to carry
wounded men out of the firing line, 28th August 1916,
aged 20. No known grave. Commemorated on the Loos
Memorial, Pas-de-Calais, France. Panel 22 to 25.
Son of Mr John and Mrs Edith Barber of 12A New Row,
Kenilworth.

BARKER, Edward Vernon *[NJ]

Private 27998, 10th Battalion, Royal Warwickshire Regiment.
Killed in action in France, 22nd March 1918. No known grave.
Commemorated on the Arras Memorial, Pas-de-Calais, France. Bay 3.
Lived at Dunn's Pit Farm, Kenilworth.

BARNETT, Henry (known as Harry) *[NJ]

Private 9016, 1st Battalion, Royal Welsh Fusiliers.
Killed in action, 19th October 1914, aged 28.
No known grave.
Commemorated on the Ypres (Menin Gate) Memorial,
Belgium. Panel 22.
Eldest son of Mr and Mrs Edward Barnett of Whitemoor,
Kenilworth.
Husband of Amy Phyllis Barnett of 6 Spring Lane, Kenilworth.

BATES, Harold Christopher *NJ

Lieutenant, Royal Engineers.
Killed in action in France, 18th August 1915, aged 24.
Buried in La Gorgue Communal Cemetery, Nord, France.
II. B 2.
Son of Mr John Halifax and Mrs Eleanor Bates of White
Thorn, Kenilworth.

BAYLISS, Frederick *N

Private 1682, 1st Battalion Warwickshire Regiment.
Killed in action, 25th April 1915, aged 24. No known grave.
Commemorated on the Ypres (Menin Gate) Memorial, Belgium. Panel 8.
Nephew of Mr William Bayliss of Mill End, Kenilworth.

BEEVERS, William *NJ

Private 280545, Queen's Own Oxfordshire Hussars.
Killed in action, 25th March 1918, aged 20. No known grave.
Commemorated on the Pozières Memorial, Somme, France. Panel 6.
Son of Mr and Mrs William Beevers of Newlands, Waverley Road, Kenilworth.

BIDMEAD, Harry Lloyd *N

Corporal 12590, 16th Battalion Lancashire Fusiliers.
Killed in action by a shell, 6th June 1918, aged 23.
Buried in Cabaret-Rouge British Cemetery, Souchez, Pas-
de-Calais, France. VIII. M. 34
Son of the late Mr and Mrs Bidmead of Warwick Road,
Kenilworth.
Sister of Mrs Buckingham, of Mount Pleasant Cottages,
 Albion Street, Kenilworth.

BOYT, H. G. R. *NJ

Second Lieutenant, 3rd Fighter Squadron, Royal Air Force.
Killed in England, 31st July 1918, on his last trial flight before leaving for France,
aged 19.
Buried in Stanhoe (All Saints) Churchyard, Norfolk.
Only son of Mr C. and Mrs E. Boyt of Charlton, Windy Arbour, Kenilworth.

BRADSHAW, John Welch *NJ

Corporal 265706, 1st/7th Battalion, Royal Warwickshire Regiment.
Killed by a sniper in France, 4th October 1917, aged 32.
No known grave. Commemorated on the Tyne Cot Memorial, Zonnebeke, West-Vlaanderen, Belgium. Panel 23 to 28 and 163A.
Son of the late Mr Bradshaw of Offchurch.
Brother of Mr W. H. Bradshaw of Warwick Road, Kenilworth.

BRICKNELL, George, MM *NJW

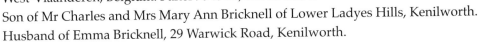

Company Sergeant Major 10088, D Company,
8th Battalion, South Staffordshire Regiment.
Awarded MM for carrying a message under heavy fire.
Killed in action, 12th October 1917, aged 37.
No known grave.
Commemorated on the Tyne Cot Memorial, Zonnebeke,
West-Vlaanderen, Belgium. Panel 90 to 92, 162 to 162A.
Son of Mr Charles and Mrs Mary Ann Bricknell of Lower Ladyes Hills, Kenilworth.
Husband of Emma Bricknell, 29 Warwick Road, Kenilworth.

BUCKINGHAM, Albert Edward *

Private 42677, D Company, 10th Battalion, Royal Warwickshire Regiment.
Died in France, 25th September 1918, aged 32. Buried in Le Touret Military
Cemetery, Richebourg-L'Avoue, Pas-de-Calais, France. IV. H. 12.
Husband of Elsie K. Buckingham, of 186 Barrows Road, Sparkhill, Birmingham.

BUCKINGHAM, Herbert *N

Uncertain of this man's identification. He was probably Edgar Herbert
Buckingham, Private 37766, 2nd/7th Battalion Royal Warwickshire Regiment.
He was born at Coventry, enlisted at Cheltenham, Gloucestershire and resided at
Coventry. Killed in action 14th April 1918. No known grave.
Commemorated on the Ploegsteert Memorial, Comines-Warneton, Hainaut,
Belgium. Panel 2 & 3.

BURTON, Charles Silvester *N

Private 28657, 10th Battalion, Royal Warwickshire Regiment.
Killed in action in France, 23rd March 1918, aged 36. No known grave.
Commemorated on the Arras Memorial, Pas-de-Calais, France. Bay 3.
Eldest son of Mr and Mrs Charles Burton of High Street, Kenilworth.

BUTLER, Charles Austin [+]

Corporal 16591, 8th Battalion, Duke of Wellington's (West Riding Regiment).
Killed in action in France, 30th September 1916, aged 24.
Buried in Regina Trench Cemetery, Grandcourt, Somme, France. IX. J. 15
Son of Mr and Mrs Butler of 125 Albion Street, Kenilworth.

BUTLER, Sidney [*N]

Private 11951, 8th Battalion, Royal Welsh Fusiliers.
Died at sea of wounds received at Gallipoli, 25th August 1915, aged 22.
Commemorated on the Helles Memorial, Turkey. Panel 77 to 80.
Son of Mr Thomas and Mrs Hannah Butler of Woodville, Lower Ladyes Hills,
Kenilworth.

CANNON, Walter [*N]

Private 20028, 6th Battalion, Dorsetshire Regiment.
Formerly 053673, Royal Army Medical Corps.
Killed in action, 8th June 1918. No known grave.
Commemorated on the Pozières Memorial, Somme, France. Panel 48.
Married, wife living at Clifton, Bristol. Born Howington, Wells, Somerset.

CARTER, Charles [*N]

Corporal 19462, 8th Battalion, South Lancashire
Regiment. Killed in action, 13th June 1917, aged 21.
No known grave.
Commemorated on the Ypres (Menin Gate) Memorial,
Belgium. Panel 37.
Son of the late Mr Harry and Mrs Charlotte Carter of
Kenilworth.

CARTER, Cyril William [*N]

Lance Corporal 18114, 5th Battalion Oxford and Bucks Light Infantry.
Killed by a shell at Passchendaele Ridge 22nd December 1917, aged 25.
No known grave.
Commemorated on the Tyne Cot Memorial, Zonnebeke, West-Vlaanderen,
Belgium. Panel 96 to 98.
Youngest son of Councillor Charles James and Mrs Mabel Ann Carter of 13/15 The
Square, Kenilworth.

CASHMORE, John (Jack) *NJ

Not yet identified. Could possibly be John Cashmore, Private 4766, 9th Battalion, Royal Warwickshire Regiment. Died 10th August 1915, aged 21. Born Shustoke, enlisted Warwick, resident of Sutton Coldfield. Commemorated on the Helles Memorial, Turkey. Panel 35 to 37. Son of Mr William Charles and Mrs Emma Cashmore of 9 Four Oaks Common Road, Four Oaks Common, Birmingham.

CAY, Albert Jaffray *NJ

Lieutenant, Q.O. Worcestershire Hussars (Worcestershire Yeomanry).
Killed in action at Oghratina, Palestine, 23rd April 1916, aged 36. No known grave.
Commemorated on the Jerusalem Memorial, Israel.
Panel 3 and 5.
Only son of Mr Albert and Mrs Annie Cay, of Woodside, Kenilworth.

CHALONER, William *N

Sergeant 6884, 5th Battalion, King's Shropshire Light Infantry.
Died of wounds received in action, 29th August, 1916, aged 34.
Buried in St. Sever Cemetery, Rouen, Seine-Maritime, France.
B. 26. 7.
Son of Mr Thomas and Mrs Mary Chaloner of 35 Moorend Street, Cheltenham.
Husband of Minnie Chaloner of Little Hills, Shurdington, Cheltenham.

CLIFFT, Charles Harold *N

Sapper 32441, 2nd Field Squadron, Royal Engineers.
Killed in action in France, 23rd March 1918, aged 25.
Buried in Grand-Seraucourt British Cemetery, Aisne, France. III. J. 2.
Eldest son of Mr and Mrs Clifft of Malthouse Lane, Kenilworth.

CLIVE, Reginald Dennis *N

Flight Sub-Lieutenant, Royal Naval Air Service.
Died as a result of a flying accident in Scotland, 10th November 1917, aged 19.
Buried in St. Nicholas' Churchyard, Kenilworth.
Son of Mr H. R. and Mrs L. E. Clive of Fieldgate Lane, Kenilworth.

COLLETT, Reginald Jack *ᴺ

Private 52926, 8th Battalion Royal Fusiliers. Formerly
11497, Royal Army Service Corps.
Killed in action at Cambrai, 24th November 1917, aged 31.
No known grave.
Commemorated on the Cambrai Memorial, Louverval,
Nord, France. Panel 3 and 4.
Seventh son of the late Mr Henry and Mrs Harriet Collett
of 65 Henry Street, Kenilworth.

COLMAN, Robert *ᴺ

Private, 2/7th Battalion, Royal Warwickshire Regiment.
Served in France.
Son of Mr and Mrs F. Colman of 51 Waverley Road, Kenilworth.
No further information.

COLOMB, George Lushington, DCM *ᴺ

Lieutenant, London Regiment.
Died 22nd November 1916, aged 27.
Buried in Gezaincourt Communal Cemetery Extension, Somme, France. I. G. 17.
Son of Mr William and Mrs Maud Colomb, of Rossleigh, Greyfriars, Co. Wicklow.
Native of Athlone. Brother of Mervyn William Colomb.

COLOMB, Mervyn William *ᴺ

Second Lieutenant, 4th Battalion London Regiment (Royal Fusiliers).
Wounded near Ypres, died in England 11th May 1915.
Buried in Aldershot Military Cemetery, Hampshire. AF. 1869
Son of Mr William and Mrs Maud Colomb of Rossleigh, Greystones, Co. Wicklow.
Resided at Kentall, Warwick Road, Kenilworth. Brother of George Lushington
Colomb.

COX, Harry *ᴺ

Sergeant 5207, 1st Battalion, Rifle Brigade.
Wounded in action near Ypres 6 July 1915 and died in
hospital at Sheffield 16th August 1915, aged 20.
Buried in St Nicholas' Churchyard, Kenilworth.
Son of Mrs Theresa Cox of 89 Henry St, Kenilworth.
Brother of Wilfred George Cox.

COX, Wilfred George [+]

Rifleman, King's Royal Rifles.
Badly wounded in action at Loos 8th April 1916.
Honourably discharged.
Died in hospital in England 31st December 1923, aged 30.
Son of Mrs Theresa Cox of 89 Henry Street, Kenilworth. Brother of Harry Cox.

DANIELLS, Wilfred George [*NJ]

Private CH/19096, 1st R.M. Battalion, R.N. Division, Royal Marine Light Infantry.
Died 13th November 1916, aged 19.
No known grave.
Commemorated on the Thiepval Memorial, Somme, France. Pier and Face 1A.

DILWORTH, Albert Edward [*NO]

Private 64401, 16th Battalion Manchester Regiment,
formerly 45856, Essex Regiment.
Killed in action 25th September 1918, age 19.
No known grave. Commemorated on the Tyne Cot
Memorial, Zonnebeke, West-Vlaanderen, Belgium.
Panel 120 to 124 and 162 to 162A and 163A.
Son of Mr and Mrs T. H. Dilworth, New Row,
Kenilworth.

DRANE, Victor Henry [*NP]

Sapper, Royal Engineers.
A former clerk at the Kenilworth Post Office.
Died at sea from pneumonia on his way home from
Mesopotamia, 23rd April 1919, aged 24.
Son of Mr and Mrs W. Drane of Henry Street, Kenilworth.

DRANE-OVERS, William John [*N]

Sergeant 9594, C Company, 11th Battalion, Royal Warwickshire Regiment.
Killed in action 19th August 1916, aged 29.
Buried in Wimereux Communal Cemetery, Pas-de-Calais, France. 1908. I. P. 20A
Son of Mr John Drane-Overs of Spring Lane Cottages, Kenilworth.
Husband of Audrey T. Overs of High Street, Carisbrooke, Isle of Wight.

DREW, James *N

Lance Corporal (Signaller) 16230, 10th Battalion, Royal Warwickshire Regiment.
Killed in action 25th March 1918, aged 22. No known grave. Commemorated on the Arras Memorial, Pas-de-Calais, France. Bay 3
Son of Mr Eli J. and Mrs Emily Drew of The Common, Kenilworth.

EALES, William Edward *NJ

Private 38654, 1st Battalion, Duke of Cornwall's Light Infantry.
Formerly 226955, A.O.C.
Killed in action at Beaucamp Ridge 22nd September 1918, aged 34.
No known grave.
Commemorated on the Vis-en-Artois Memorial, Pas-de-Calais, France. Panel 6.
Son of Mr William Henry and Mrs Maria Eales.
Husband of Helen Eales, 55 Waverley Road, Kenilworth.

EDMOND, Henry Oliver *NJ

Private 581, Royal Army Medical Corps.
Died at Coventry from pneumonia 23rd October 1918, aged 28.
Buried in Kenilworth Cemetery. B. 943.
Eldest son of the late Mr and Mrs S. Edmond.
Husband of Alice Edmond.

ELLIS, Harry *N

Private, Durham Light Infantry.
Discharged through illness on service 1918. Died 26th July 1919, aged 32.
Husband of Annie Ellis, Clinton Lane, Kenilworth.
Buried in St Nicholas' Churchyard, Kenilworth.

EWEN, Donald *N

Private 1833, 1st/14th Battalion, London Regiment (London Scottish).
Killed by a sniper in France, 13th October 1915, aged 28.
No known grave.
Commemorated on the Loos Memorial, Pas-de-Calais, France. Panel 132
Son of Mr T. B. and Mrs Janet Ewen of Haslemere, Blackwell, Bromsgrove, Worcs.

FAXON, Hubert Richard *

Driver 69940, 76th Battery, Royal Field Artillery.
Died in hospital in Mesopotamia, 30th August, 1916.
Buried in Baghdad (North Gate) War Cemetery. XXI. H. 17.
Son of Mr Richard and Mrs Eva Marion Faxon, School Lane, Kenilworth.

FENERAN, Frank Edward *N

Captain, The King's (Liverpool Regiment).
Died 10th March 1915, aged 33. No known grave.
Commemorated on Le Touret Memorial, Pas-de-Calais, France. Panels 6 to 8.
Son of the late Lt. Col. Edward and Mrs Caroline Elizabeth Feneran.

FRAZER, Ernest Alfred *NM

Private 265270, 1st/7th Battalion, Royal Warwickshire
Regiment.
Killed by a sniper, 27th August 1917, aged 21.
No known grave.
Commemorated on the Tyne Cot Memorial, Zonnebeke,
West-Vlaanderen, Belgium. Panel 23 to 28 and 163A.
Son of Mr and Mrs Isaac Frazer of 13 Albion Street,
Kenilworth.
Brother of George Henry Frazer.

FRAZER, George Henry *N

Private G/21475, 7th Battalion, Queen's Own (Royal West Kent Regiment).
Formerly 24963, Gloucestershire Regiment. Died 21st September 1918, aged 31.
No known grave.
Commemorated on the Vis-en-Artois Memorial, Pas-de-Calais, France. Panel 7.
Son of Mr and Mrs Isaac Frazer of 13 Albion Street, Kenilworth.
Husband of Eliza Frazer of 4 Regent Street, Cubbington.
Brother of Ernest Alfred Frazer.

GARDNER, Henry Victor *N

Corporal 2025, 1st/7th Battalion, Royal Warwickshire
Regiment. Killed in action 18th August 1916, aged 20.
No known grave. Commemorated on the Thiepval
Memorial, Somme, France. Pier and Face 9A , 9B and 10B.
Son of Mrs Rose Yates of 8 Spring Lane, Kenilworth.

GARRETT, John *N

Gunner 34489, 'A' Battery, 282nd Brigade, Royal Field
Artillery. Killed in action 5th September 1917, aged 31.
Buried in Dozinghem Military Cemetery, Westvleteren,
Poperinge,West-Vlaanderen, Belgium. IV. F. 10
Son of Mr and Mrs George Garrett of Crimscote, Stratford-
on-Avon. Husband of Edith Timms (formerly Garrett) of 4
Spring Lane, Kenilworth.

GILKS, Arthur *NJ

(Recorded as Arthur but name seems to be Albert) Private 37967, 11th Battalion,
Royal Warwickshire Regiment. Died 27th January, 1918, aged 19. Buried in St Sever
Cemetery Extension, Rouen, France. P. VI. G. 11B. Son of Mr Samuel and Mrs
Maria Gilks of Finley Hill Cottages, Hatton, Warwick.

GILLAM, Albert Edward *N

Private 25169, 8th Battalion, East Surrey Regiment.
Killed by shell fire,1st December 1917, aged 28.
Buried in Bleuet Farm Cemetery, Elverdinghe, West-
Vlaanderen, Belgium. II. B. 23.
Son of Mr John C. and Mrs Alice Gillam of Duns Tew,
Deddington, Oxford. Husband of Agnes Gillam of 30
Spring Lane, Kenilworth.

GRAINGER, William Henry *N

Private 18045, 14th Battalion, Royal Warwickshire Regiment.
Killed in action 13th April 1918, aged 26. No known grave.
Commemorated at Ploegsteert Memorial, Comines-Warneton, Hainaut, Belgium.
Panel 2 and 3. Son of the late Mr David Grainger and Mrs A. Stanley (formerly
Grainger) of Moat Farm Cottages, Honiley, Kenilworth.

GREEN, Arthur Edward *NW

Private 50766, 10th Battalion, Royal Warwickshire
Regiment. Killed by shell fire 21st October 1918, aged 19.
Buried in Romeries Communal Cemetery Extension,
Nord, France. VI. E. 4. Youngest son of Mr David and
Mrs Louisa Green of 50 Spring Lane, Kenilworth. Brother
of Leonard Harry Green.

GREEN, Leonard Harry *[NO]

Private 16644, 9th Battalion, Royal Warwickshire Regiment.
Killed by a sniper in Mesopotamia 18th January, 1917, aged 23.
Buried in Amara War Cemetery, Iraq. XXIV. B. 16.
Son of Mr David and Mrs Louisa Green of 50 Spring Lane, Kenilworth.
Brother of Arthur E. Green.

GREGORY, Charles Howard *[N]

Lance Bombardier 126811, 'B' Battery, 165th Brigade, Royal Field Artillery.
Died of influenza in Wimereux Hospital, France, 24th October 1918, aged 22.
Buried in Terlincthun British Cemetery, Wimille, Pas-de-Calais, France. VI. B. 45.
Son of Mr James and Mrs Carrie Gregory, 21 School Lane, Kenilworth.

HARRIS, James *[NP]

Private 5893, 2nd Battalion South Staffordshire Regiment.
Killed in action 3rd February 1918, aged 34.
Buried in Metz-en-Couture Communal Cemetery British
Extension, Pas-de-Calais, France. II. G. 21.
Son of Mr Charles and Mrs Elizabeth Harris of
Birmingham. Husband of Elizabeth Harris of 42 Henry St,
Kenilworth.

HARRIS, Richard Henry *[NJM]

Private 242775, 2nd/6th Battalion, Royal Warwickshire Regiment.
Died 3rd April 1918, aged 36.
No known grave.
Commemorated on the Pozières Memorial, Somme, France. Panel 18 and 19.
Son of Mr Charles and Mrs Annie Harris of St John's Street, Kenilworth.
He was married and also lived in St John's Street.

HAZEL, Arthur William *[N]

Sergeant 16826, Royal Warwickshire Regiment.
Severely wounded and discharged 20th July 1918.
Died at Northfield Sanatorium, Birmingham 28th July 1919, aged 29.
Buried in St Nicholas' Churchyard, Kenilworth.
Son of Mrs Elizabeth Hazel of 8 New Row, Kenilworth.

HEWITT, Frank *N

Lance Corporal 22778, 4th Royal Warwickshire Regiment.
Injured April 1917, died at Hollymoor Military Hospital,
Northfield, Birmingham 15th August 1919, aged 21.
Buried in St Nicholas' Churchyard, Kenilworth.
Second son of Mr Harry and Mrs Sarah Georgina Hewitt
of Mill End, Kenilworth.
Brother of William Charles Hewitt.

HEWITT, William Charles *N

Rifleman 5449, 1st Battalion, Rifle Brigade.
Killed in action in France, 19th December 1914, aged 18.
No known grave.
Commemorated on the Ploegsteert Memorial, Comines-
Warneton, Hainut, Belgium. Panel 10.
Also commemorated on his brother Frank's gravestone in
St Nicholas' Churchyard, Kenilworth.
Eldest son of Mr Harry and Mrs Sarah Georgina Hewitt
of Mill End, Kenilworth. Brother of Frank Hewitt.

HICKMAN Thomas William *NM

Private 21861, 8th Battalion, Royal Berkshire Regiment.
Killed in action in France 18th August 1916, aged 27.
No known grave.
Commemorated on the Thiepval Memorial, Somme, France. Pier and Face 11D.
Elder son of Mr and Mrs Hickman of Mill End, Kenilworth.

HINCKS, Harry *ND

Private 34023, 1st Battalion, Duke of Cornwall's Light
Infantry. Formerly 20108, Royal Warwickshire Regiment.
Killed in action 8th May 1917, aged 39.
No known grave.
Commemorated on the Arras Memorial, Pas-de-Calais,
France. Bay 6.
Married with two children.
Kenilworth butcher with shops in Warwick Road, Kenilworth.

HOPKINS, Ernest H. *^N

Private 15693, 3rd Battalion, Coldstream Guards.
Killed in action 13th April 1918, aged 26.
Buried in Merville Communal Cemetery Extension,
Nord, France. I. D. 40.
Son of Mr H. and Mrs S. A. Hopkins of 17 Henry Street,
Kenilworth.

HORSLEY, Christopher *^N

Private 2142, 1st/7th Royal Warwickshire Regiment.
Died in Coventry Barracks December 1914, aged 18.
Buried in Coventry Cemetery.
Nephew of Mr and Mrs Upton of Albion Street,
Kenilworth. His parents lived at Ratley, Warwickshire,
where he is also recorded on the war memorial.

HUBBARD, Arthur James *^N

Private 310550, 'B' Squadron, Warwickshire Yeomanry.
Wounded in action at Gaza, died in hospital at
Alexandria 24th April, 1917, aged 27.
Buried in Alexandria (Hadra) War Memorial Cemetery,
Egypt. D. 103.
Son of Mr Martin and Mrs Sarah Hubbard of 25
Stoneleigh Road, Kenilworth.

INSALL, Samuel Henry *^N

Private 8450, 2nd Battalion, Oxford and Bucks Light
Infantry. Killed in action 6th April 1915, aged 19.
Buried in Brown's Road Military Cemetery, Festubert,
France. VIII F. 4.
Eldest son of Mr and Mrs Sam Insall of Whitemoor,
Kenilworth.

JAKEMAN, William Alfred *^N

Private 24655, 2nd/7th Warwickshire Regiment.
Killed in action 22nd November 1918, aged 22.
Buried in Cambrai East Military Cemetery, France. III. A. 57.
Son of Mr and Mrs Jakeman of Norton Lindsey.

KIDD, Guy Egerton, DSO *N

Major, 'A' Battery, 70th Brigade, Royal Field Artillery.
Killed in action 26th September 1916.
Buried in Flatiron Copse Cemetery, Mametz, Somme, France. II. F. 5.
Eldest son of Dr Percy Kidd of 60 Brook Street, London, W.
Major Kidd was married and resided at Ladbrook House, New Street, Kenilworth prior to the war.

LAKE, Arthur +

Sergeant 888, 10th Battalion, Royal Warwickshire Regiment.
Killed in action 21st October 1918, aged 30. No known grave.
Commemorated on the Vis-en-Artois Memorial, Pas-de-Calais, France. Panel 3.
Son of Mr Robert and Mrs Jane Lake of Albion Street, Kenilworth.
Brother of Mrs Colley of 22 Waterloo Street, Hillfields, Coventry.

LETTS, Ernest *N

Private 36676, 1st/4th Battalion, Gloucestershire
Regiment. Formerly 19283 Royal Warwickshire Regiment.
Killed in action 9th October 1917, aged 31.
Buried in Poelcapelle British Cemetery, Langemark-
Poelcapelle, West-Vlaanderen, Belgium. IV. A. 2.
Husband of Ada Letts of 65 Henry Street, Kenilworth.

LIGGINS, Gilbert Percy *NJ

Lance Sergeant 5402, 16th (The Queen's) Lancers.
Killed in action 21st February 1915, aged 30
No known grave.
Commemorated on the Ypres (Menin Gate) Memorial,
Belgium. Panel 5.
Son of the late Mr Joseph and Mrs Emma S. Liggins of
Stoneleigh Road, Kenilworth.
Husband of Mrs Liggins of Windy Arbour, Kenilworth.

MANTON, Harry *N

Private PLY/2454(S), Royal Marine Light Infantry.
Taken prisoner and died at Valenciennes, 29th August 1918, aged 22.
Buried in Valenciennes (St Roch) Communal Cemetery, Nord, France.V. G. 9
Husband of Mrs Manton of Spring Lane, Kenilworth.

MARTIN, Austin *N

Private 153, 1st Battalion, Royal Warwickshire Regiment.
Wounded in action 6th October 1914, died from the
effects 15th June 1920, aged 34.
Buried in Kenilworth Cemetery. C. 1014.
Son of Mr Edward and Mrs Elizabeth Martin, 34 Spring
Lane, Kenilworth. Husband of Minnie Martin, 51 Albion
Street, Kenilworth. Brother of Charles James W. Martin.

MARTIN, Charles James W. *NP

Sergeant 82985, 34th Battalion, Machine Gun Corps (Inf).
Formerly 16398 Royal Warwickshire Regiment.
Killed in action 14th October 1918, aged 22.
Buried in Hooge Crater Cemetery, Ypres, West-
Vlaanderen, Belgium. XVII. L. 12.
Youngest son of Mr Edward and Mrs Elizabeth Martin, 34
Spring Lane, Kenilworth. Brother of Austin Martin.

MARTIN, Harold Charles *NJP

Lance Corporal 25388, 14th Battalion, Gloucestershire Regiment.
Killed by a sniper 2nd May 1916, aged 25.
Buried in Merville Communal Cemetery, Nord, France. VI. P. 31.
Son Mr Joseph and Mrs Fanny Martin, of 16 Wills Street, Lozells, Birmingham.
Member of Kenilworth Post Office staff.

MARVIN, James *N

Sapper 198033, 180th Tunnelling Company, Royal Engineers.
Killed in action 6th January 1918, aged 34.
Buried in Epehy Wood Farm Cemetery, Epehy, Somme, France. V. C. 5.
Son of Mr Owen and Mrs Ellen Marvin of Durless. Husband of Ellen Marvin, of
Durless, Kilsallagh, Westport, Co. Mayo, Ireland.

MATTHEWS, William Charles *N

Rifleman 44352, 11th Battalion, Royal Irish Rifles.
Died 2nd March 1917, aged 40.
Buried in Boulogne Eastern Cemetery, Pas-de-Calais, France. VIII. A. 197.
Son of Mr George and Mrs Mary Matthews of Leamington Spa; husband of
Beatrice Emma Matthews, 78 Doggett Road, Catford, London.

McCOUSINS, William Henry *N

Private 202294, 5th Battalion, Royal Warwickshire
Regiment, Labour Corps. Formerly 6961 Royal
Warwickshire Regiment.
Died from pneumonia, 12th February 1918.
Buried in Lijssenthoek Military Cemetery, Poperinge,
West-Vlaanderen, Belgium. XXVII. FF. 19A
Lived at 38 New Street, Kenilworth.

MITCHINER, George *NJ

Rifleman A/3702, 10th Battalion, King's Royal Rifle
Corps. Died 12th December 1915, aged 19.
Buried in Etaples Military Cemetery, Pas-de-Calais,
France. VI. A. 17A.
Son of Mr Thomas and Mrs Elizabeth Mitchiner, 182
Warwick Road, Kenilworth. Brother of Harry Mitchiner.

MITCHINER, Harry *NJ

Able Seaman 235318, H.M.S. Hampshire, Royal Navy.
Drowned in H.M.S. Hampshire, 5th June 1916, aged 26.
Commemorated on the Portsmouth Naval Memorial,
Hampshire. 13.
Second son of Mr Thomas and Mrs Elizabeth Mitchiner,
182 Warwick Road, Kenilworth.
Brother of George Mitchiner.

MORGAN John Charles *N

Private 22464, 10th Battalion, Royal Warwickshire Regiment.
Died 10th June 1917, aged 34.
Buried in Monthuon Military Cemetery, Le Tréport, Seine-Maritime, France.
III. H. 5A. Husband of Annie Morgan of 104 Albion Street, Kenilworth.

MOWBRAY, Charles *NJM

Private 4785, 2nd/7th Battalion, Royal Warwickshire Regiment.
Died of meningitis in hospital in France 8th January 1917, aged 27.
Buried in Hem Communal Cemetery, Somme, France. C. 4.
Son of Mr William and Mrs Hannah Mowbray of 45 St John's Terrace, Kenilworth.

MOWE, Jesse *NM

Gunner 840482, 'D' Battery, 307th Brigade, Royal Field Artillery.
Wounded in action 8th December 1916.
Died in hospital at Rouen, 3rd January 1917, aged 20.
Buried in St Sever Cemetery Extension, Rouen, Seine-Maritime, France O. IV. G. 10
Son of Mr and Mrs W. Mowe of Kenilworth.

MULCAHY, Frederick Daniel *N

Private 60880, 12th/13th Battalion, Northumberland
Fusiliers.
Died 25th October 1918, aged 36.
Buried in Awoingt British Cemetery, Nord, France. II. D. 11.
Son of Mr Daniel and Mrs Katherine Mulcahy of London.
Husband of Ada Mulcahy, 60 Furley Street, Peckham,
London.

NEWEY, Charles William *N

Private 26063, 2nd Battalion, Worcestershire Regiment.
Died 11th April 1918, aged 38. No known grave.
Commemorated on the Ploegsteert Memorial, Comines-Warneton, Hainaut,
Belgium. Panel 5.
Son of Mr Charles and Mrs Emma Newey of 11 New Row, Kenilworth.
Husband of Bertha Rose Newey of St Kilda, 16 Greville Road, Emscote, Warwick.

NIXON, Alfred George *N

Fitter Staff Sergeant 16564, 24th Brigade HQ, Royal Field Artillery.
Died 17th July 1918, aged 38.
Buried in Nine Elms British Cemetery, Poperinghe, West-Vlaanderen, Belgium.
XV. A. 11.
Third son of Mr Ernest Eli and Mrs Annie Nixon of High Street, Kenilworth.
Husband of Mildred W. Nixon, 27 High Street, Kenilworth.

OVERTON, Albert Ernest *N

Sergeant 1193, 2nd Battalion, Royal Warwickshire Regiment.
Killed in action 25th September 1915, aged 26. No known grave.
Commemorated on the Loos Memorial, Pas-de-Calais, France. Panel 22 to 25.
Son of Mr and Mrs John Overton, 72 Henry Street, Kenilworth.

PARKYN, Leonard Norman [+]

Private, 2nd Rifle Brigade, King's Royal Rifle Corps.
Wounded in action and taken prisoner March 1918.
Released January 1919. In hospital in Scotland until July
1919. Died at home 13th August 1920.
Youngest son of Mr and Mrs W. Parkyn of Pleasaunce
Farm Cottages, Kenilworth. Brother of William Jacob
Parkyn.

PARKYN, William Jacob [*N]

Private 242560, 6th Battalion, Royal Warwickshire
Regiment.
Killed in action 27th August 1917, aged 22.
Buried in Tyne Cot Cemetery, Zonnebeke, West-
Vlaanderen, Belgium. VIII H. 12.
Son of Mr and Mrs W. Parkyn of Pleasaunce Farm
Cottages, Kenilworth. Brother of Leonard Norman
Parkyn.

PITTAWAY, Frederick Howlett [*NJ]

Private 30061, 2nd Battalion, Royal Warwickshire Regiment.
Died 3rd September 1916, aged 27. No known grave.
Commemorated on the Thiepval Memorial, Somme, France.
Pier and Face 9A, 9B and 10B.
Son of Mr William and Mrs Susan Pittaway of St John's Terrace, Kenilworth.

PLANT, Francis [*N]

Chief Petty Officer 117099(CH), H.M.S. Natal, Royal Navy.
Lost off Cromarty when his ship blew up January 1916, aged 52.
Cromarty Cemetery, Ross and Cromarty. K. North-East 17.

PRATT, E. Joseph [*NM]

Regimental Sergeant Major 2469, 10th Battalion, Royal Warwickshire Regiment.
Died of wounds received in action 20th September 1917, aged 41.
Buried in Bus House Cemetery, Voormezele, Ypres, West-Vlaanderen, Belgium.
1. 7.
Lived with his parents for many years at Washbrook House and later in New
Street, Kenilworth. Married Miss Bayliss a teacher at St Nicholas' School.

RAWLINS, Walter Thomas *N

Private 33584, 11th Battalion, Border Regiment.
Killed by a sniper 14th April 1917, aged 38. No known grave.
Commemorated on the Thiepval Memorial, Somme, France.
Pier and Face 6A and 7C.
Son of the late Mr Francis Rawlins, of 80 Priory Road, Kenilworth.

REED, Charles Sydney *N

Second Lieutenant, 7th Battalion, Leicestershire Regiment.
Killed in action 14th July 1916, aged 29. No known grave.
Commemorated on the Thiepval Memorial, Somme, France. Pier & Face 2C, 3A.
Only son of Mr Charles and Mrs Alice Margaret Reed of Prior's Field Cottages,
Malthouse Lane, Kenilworth.

REEVE, Alfred *NJ

Private 4733, 1st/7th Battalion, Royal Warwickshire Regiment.
Killed in action 25th July 1916, aged 32. No known grave.
Commemorated on the Thiepval Memorial, Somme, France.
Pier and Face 9A, 9B and 10B.
Son of Mr Edwin and Mrs Lucy Reeve of Warwick Road, Kenilworth.
Married with six children and lived at Fairview Place, Kenilworth.
Brother of Leonard Henry Reeve, DCM.

REEVE, Edward *NJ

Driver TS/1215, Royal Army Service Corps.
Died in Holmington Hospital, London, 13th September 1914.
Buried in East London Cemetery, Plaistow, Essex. 10647.
Son of Mr Robert and Mrs Elizabeth Reeve, of Gt. Burstead, Essex.
Second whip to the North Warwickshire hunt.

REEVE, Leonard Henry, DCM *NJ

Corporal 11935, 2nd Battalion, King's Royal Rifle Corps.
Killed by gas poisoning 18th July 1916, aged 24.
Buried in Heilly Station Cemetery, Mericourt-L'Abbe,
Somme, France. II. D. 13.
Son of Mr Edwin and Mrs Lucy Reeve of Warwick Road,
Kenilworth. Brother of Alfred Reeve.

REYNOLDS, Harry *NWO

Private 45219, 14th Battalion, Durham Light
Infantry.
Formerly S2/018350, Royal Army Service Corps.
Died 3rd December 1917, aged 38. No known grave.
Commemorated on the Cambrai Memorial,
Louverval, Nord, France. Panel 10.
Married with 2 children, and lived at 25 School
Lane, Kenilworth.

REYNOLDS, James *N

Private 22782, 11th Battalion, Royal Warwickshire Regiment.
Killed in action 28th April 1917. No known grave.
Commemorated on the Arras Memorial, Pas-de-Calais, France. Bay 3.
Born Kinton, Staffs. Lived at Kenilworth.

RIVERS, Carlton *NJ

Private 71142, 43rd Company, Machine Gun Corps.
Formerly 21600, Somerset Light Infantry.
Killed in action 22nd August 1917, aged 25. No known grave.
Commemorated on the Tyne Cot Memorial, Zonnebeke, West-Vlaanderen,
Belgium. Panel 154 to 159 and 163A.
Only son of Mr Leonard and Mrs Margaret Rivers of Freza, Waverley Road,
Kenilworth.

ROBERTSON, William *N

No further information.
Could possibly be William Robertson, Private 13605, 12th (Service) Battalion,
Hampshire Regiment.
Formerly Private 7818 Royal Warwickshire Regiment.
Killed in action 24th April 1917 in the Balkans, aged 28.
Commemorated on the Dorian Memorial, Greece.
Born in Birmingham.
Son of Mr David and Mrs Clara Robertson, 55 Leamington Road, Sparkbrook.
Husband of Mrs Catherine Clayton Robertson of 14 Coronation Place, Aston
Manor, Birmingham.

RUDDOCK, Harold *N

No further information.

SABIN, Frank *NM

Private 3688, 2nd Battalion, Royal Warwickshire Regiment.
Killed in action 25th September 1915, aged 30. No known grave.
Commemorated on the Loos Memorial, Pas-de-Calais, France. Panel 22 to 25.
Born and lived in Leamington.
Son of Mr John Sabin of 60 Salisbury Road, Gloucester.

SADLER, Arthur Albert*NJD

Bombardier 614314, 15th (Warwick) Brigade, Royal Horse Artillery.
Killed in action 30th August 1917, aged 26.
Buried in Duhallow A.D.S. Cemetery, Ypres, West-Vlaanderen, Belgium. VII. B. 13.
Husband of Violet Sadler of 5 St John's Avenue, Kenilworth.

SAWYER, Arthur *NM

Private 1137, 2nd Battalion, Royal Warwickshire
Regiment.
Killed in action 7th November 1914, aged 23.
No known grave.
Commemorated on the Ypres (Menin) Gate Memorial,
Belgium. Panel 8.
Eldest son of the late Mr William Sawyer and Mrs Mary
Sawyer of 84 Clinton Lane, Kenilworth.

SEEKINGS, Laurie *N

Bombardier 74718, 'E' Battery, Royal Horse Artillery.
Wounded in France August 1915. Died from appendicitis
at hospital in Eastbourne, 28th September 1915, aged 18.
Buried in Kenilworth Cemetery. B. 686.
Son of Mr Harry and Mrs Jessica Seekings, 8 Barrowell
Terrace, Kenilworth.

SEYMOUR, Constance Emily Mary *N

Probationer Nurse 83/7564, Queen Alexandra's Imperial Military Nursing Service.
Died at the Connaught Hospital, Aldershot 12th February 1917, aged 29.
Buried in Aldershot Military Cemetery, Hampshire. AG. 383.
Daughter of Lord and Lady Ernest Seymour of The Firs, Kenilworth.

SKELSEY, Alfred *N

Corporal 15709, 7th Battalion, Yorkshire Regiment.
Died at the 3rd Western General Hospital, Cardiff, from gun shot wounds received in action, 28th August 1916, aged 41.
Buried in St Nicholas' Churchyard, Kenilworth.
Son of Mr William and Mrs Harriett Skelsey of Albion Street, Kenilworth.

SMITH, Herbert James *N

Sapper 43894, 18th Signal Company, Royal Engineers.
Killed in action 13th July 1916, aged 19. No known grave.
Commemorated on the Thiepval Memorial, Somme,
France. Pier and Face 8 A and 8 D.
Second son of Mr and Mrs Edwin Smith of Mill End,
Kenilworth.

SMITH, William James *N

Lance Corporal 9991, 1st Battalion, Cheshire Regiment.
Killed in action 15th September 1914, aged 23. No known grave.
Commemorated on the La Ferté-sous-Jouarre Memorial, Seine-et-Marne, France.
Nephew of Mr R. Biddle of Henry Street, Kenilworth.

SPICER, Arthur Henry *N

Private 201676, 2nd Battalion, Royal Warwickshire Regiment.
Died of pneumonia at Turin 25th May 1918, aged 32.
Buried in Turin Town Cemetery, Italy.
Son of Mr Arthur Henry and Mrs Elizabeth Spicer, 78 Warwick Road, Kenilworth.

STANLEY, Harry +

Private, 2/6th Royal Warwickshire Regiment.
Served in France. Died in the Ministry of Pensions Hospital, Leicester, 5th September 1923, aged 43. Lived at High Street, Kenilworth.

STANLEY, James Thomas *NJ

Private 1618, 2nd Battalion, Royal Warwickshire
Regiment. Killed in action 12th November 1914, aged 22.
Buried in Poperinge Old Military Cemetery, West-
Vlaanderen, Belgium. I. L. 65. Son of Mr George and
Mrs Ellen Stanley, of Bulkington Cottages, Kenilworth.
Husband of Frances Amelia King (formerly Stanley) of 27
Queen's Road, Peckham, London. Brother of John Stanley.

STANLEY, John +

Private G/29153, Queen's Own (Royal West Kent Regiment).
Formerly 43040 Hampshire Regiment.
Killed in action 22nd August, 1918, aged 19.
Buried in Beacon Cemetery, Sailly-Laurette, Somme, France. VI. J. 5.
Son of Mr George and Mrs Ellen Stanley of Bulkington Cottages, Kenilworth.
Brother of James Thomas Stanley.

SWANN, George Henry *NJ

Private 21045, 10th Battalion, Worcestershire Regiment.
Killed in action 3rd July 1916, aged 31. No known grave.
Commemorated on the Thiepval Memorial, Somme, France. Pier & Face 5 A, 6 C.
Son of Mr William and Mrs Mercy Ann Swann, 1 Cross Row, Warwick Road,
Kenilworth.

TAYLOR, F. E. *N

No further information.
Possibly Frederick C. Taylor, Private 17946, 16th Battalion, Royal Warwickshire
Regiment. Killed in action 7th October 1917, France & Flanders.
Buried in Reservoir Cemetery, Ypres, West-Vlaanderen, Belgium. IX. H. 26.
Born Stratford-upon-Avon, enlisted Leamington, resided at New Cubbington.

THOMPSON, Edgar *N

Rifleman C/6391, 18th Battalion, King's Royal Rifle Corps.
Killed in action 15th September 1916, aged 22. No known grave.
Commemorated on the Thiepval Memorial, Somme, France. Pier & Face 13 A, 13 B.
Son of Mr W. A. Thompson of Priory Road, Kenilworth.
His twin brother was in the same battalion.

TOOKEY, James Presley *NO

Private 266230, 1st/7th Battalion, Royal Warwickshire Regiment.
Killed in action at Passchendaele 4th October 1917,
attempting to save his officer, aged 36.
No known grave.
Commemorated on the Tyne Cot Memorial, Zonnebeke,
West-Vlaanderen, Belgium. Panel 23 to 28 and 163A.
Husband of Jessie Mansell Mary Tookey of 26 Spring
Lane, Kenilworth.

TWEEDY, Reginald Carlyon *ND

Major, Royal Army Medical Corps.
Died at Newquay 12th July 1917.
Buried in St Kenwyn churchyard, Kenwyn, Cornwall.
Husband of Edith J. Tweedy, of Hyde House, Waterloo Place, Leamington Spa.
Father of Trevor Carlyon Tweedy.
General practitioner in Kenilworth.

TWEEDY, Trevor Carlyon *N

Captain, 6th Battalion, Northumberland Fusiliers.
Killed in action 15th September 1916, aged 21.
Buried in Delville Wood Cemetery, Longueval, Somme, France. XXX. L. 4.
Elder son of Major Reginald Carlyon Tweedy, RAMC, and Mrs Edith J. Tweedy of
Abbey House, Abbey Hill, Kenilworth.

VINCENT, Edgar Arthur *NJM

Private 23724, 16th Battalion, Royal Warwickshire
Regiment.
Killed in action 10th May 1917, aged 20.
No known grave.
Commemorated on the Arras Memorial, Pas-de-Calais,
France. Bay 3.
Son of Mr Edward and Mrs Charlotte Vincent of 10
White's Row, Warwick Road, Kenilworth.

WALTON, Spencer *NJ

Private 42466, 11th Battalion, Suffolk Regiment.
Formerly TR/9/34829, T.R.
Died 23rd August 1918, aged 19.
Buried in Aire Communal Cemetery, Pas-de-Calais, France. IV. C. 3.
Son of Mr John and Mrs Amy L. Walton of Windy Arbour, Kenilworth.

WARD, Norman John *NJ

Second Lieutenant, 11th Battalion, Royal Warwickshire Regiment.
Killed in action 11th August 1916, aged 21. No known grave.
Commemorated on the Thiepval Memorial, Somme, France. Pier & Face 9 A B, 10B.
Only son of Mr John James and Mrs Amelia Ann Ward of Glencoe, Barrow Road,
Kenilworth.

WARD, William George *NJ

Private 30148, 2nd Battalion, Hampshire Regiment.
Wounded in action 26th September 1918, died in the Cambridge Hospital,
Aldershot, 26th February 1919, aged 19.
Buried in Kenilworth Cemetery. C. 854.
Son of Mr George E. and Mrs Emma Ward of 22 St John's Street, Kenilworth.

WARREN, Harvey *N

Private 19461, 2nd Battalion, South Lancashire Regiment.
Killed in action 28th October 1918, aged 36.
Buried in Pommereuil British Cemetery, Nord, France.
B. 1.
Husband of Lucy Warren of 18 Clinton Lane, Kenilworth.

WATSON, William Henry *N

Private 16122, 1st Battalion, Royal Warwickshire Regiment.
Formerly 1871, Royal Army Service Corps.
Killed in action 23rd October 1916.
Buried in Thiepval Anglo-French Cemetery, Authuille, Somme, France. II. F. 7.
Grandson of Mrs Watson of Henry Street, Kenilworth.

WEBB, Frank *NJ

Corporal, 1st Life Guards. Served in France.
No further information.
Could possibly be Frank Webb, Sergeant 12757, 11th Battalion, Royal Warwickshire
Regiment. Killed in action 26th April 1917, aged 29.
Buried in Duisans British Cemetery, Etrum, Pas-de-Calais, France.
Son of Mr Thomas and Mrs Jane Webb, Hearsall Common, Canley Gates, Coventry.

WEBB, William *N

Private 42325, Somerset Light Infantry.
Died at the Military Hospital, Belfast, 19th July 1918.
Buried in Belfast City Cemetery, County Antrim. H. 538.
Born Fulham, Middlesex, enlisted in Kenilworth.

WEBSTER, Edward John *NJ

Private 45719, 2nd/4th Battalion, Hampshire Regiment.
Killed in action 13th September, 1918, aged 19.
Buried in Hermies Hill British Cemetery, Pas-de-Calais,
France. II. E. 4.
Eldest son of Mr Edward Wheeler and Mrs Ellen J.
Webster of 2 White's Row, Kenilworth.

WEBSTER, Robert George *N

Private 66141, 80th Field Ambulance, Royal Army Medical Corps.
Served in France and Salonika. Killed whilst carrying a wounded comrade to
safety, 9th May 1917, aged 20.
Buried in Doiran Military Cemetery, Greece. VI. C. 16.
Son of Mr William Wheeler and Mrs Edith Webster of 42 Warwick Road,
Kenilworth. Native of Rugby.

WEST, William James +

Private, 3rd Royal Warwickshire Regiment.
Discharged medically unfit for further service and died in Hatton Asylum,
Warwick, 2nd November 1917.

WEYMAN, John W. +

Private 1261, 'E' Company, 1st/6th Battalion, Royal Welsh Fusiliers.
Killed in action at Sulva Bay 10th August 1915, aged 25. No known grave.
Commemorated on the Helles Memorial, Turkey. Panel 77 to 80.
Son of Mr and Mrs J. Weyman of Gwern-y-Felin, Henryd, Conway,
Caernarvonshire. Husband of Margaret Weyman of 7 Hammond's Terrace, Clinton
Lane, Kenilworth.

WHATELEY, Edward *N

Lance Corporal 14040, 8th Battalion, South Staffordshire
Regiment. Killed in action 10th July 1916. No known
grave. Commemorated on the Thiepval Memorial,
Somme, France. Pier and Face 7B.
Son of Mrs Whateley, of Castle Green, Kenilworth.
Married with one child and living at Castle Green,
Kenilworth. Brother of Thomas William Whateley.

WHATELEY, Thomas William *N

Rifleman, R/17169, 13th Battalion, King's Royal
Rifle Corps.
Killed in action, 1st August 1916. Buried in Flatiron
Copse Cemetery, Mametz, France. IX. G. 10.
Son of Mrs Whateley, of Castle Green, Kenilworth.
Husband of Mrs B. J. Whateley, of 93 Henry Street,
Kenilworth. Brother of Edward Whateley.

WHITE, Dudley Nevill *N

Corporal 200865, 'D' Battalion, Tank Corps.
Formerly 32209, Machine Gun Corps.
Killed in action 9th October 1917, aged 20.
No known grave.
Commemorated on the Tyne Cot Memorial, Zonnebeke,
West-Vlaanderen, Belgium. Panel 159 to 160.
Son of Mr Frederick Charles and Mrs Lucy White of
Castle Rest, Kenilworth.

WILKSHIRE, Frederick Richard *N

Lance Sergeant, R/3718, 11th Battalion, King's Royal Rifle
Corps.
Killed in action 4th April 1917, aged 20.
Buried in Bancourt British Cemetery, Pas-de-Calais,
France. II. G. I.
Son of Mr Charles Wilkshire of Bridge Street, Kenilworth.
Brother of William Wilkshire.

WILKSHIRE, William *N

Private 498, 1st Battalion, Royal Warwickshire Regiment.
Killed in action 25th April 1915, aged 33.
No known grave.
Commemorated on the Ypres (Menin Gate) Memorial,
Belgium. Panel 8.
Son of Mr Charles Wilkshire of Bridge Street, Kenilworth.
Brother of Frederick R. Wilkshire.

WILMOT, Sacheverel Darwin *N

Captain, 159th Siege Battery, Royal Garrison Artillery.
Served in Mesopotamia. Died of influenza in Karachi Military Hospital 14th
October 1918, aged 33.
Buried in Karachi Cemetery. A/E B. 7.
Commemorated on the Delhi Memorial (India Gate), India. Face 1.
Son of Rev. and Mrs Darwin Wilmot of Castle Hill, Kenilworth. Husband of Annie
Dudley Wilmot of Trevena, Lower Bourne, Farnham, Surrey.

WINSTANLEY, Oswald Coke *N

Second Lieutenant, 5th Battalion, Welsh Regiment.
Killed in action 10th August 1915, aged 27. No known grave.
Commemorated on the Helles Memorial, Turkey. Panel 140 to 144.
Son of the late Mr George and Mrs Harriett Coke Winstanley of Crackley Hall,
Kenilworth.

Appendix II: Those who died in (or as a result of) the Great War, but are not commemorated on the War Memorial

BATERBEE, George

Private, 9th Norfolk Regiment.
Served in France and wounded. Discharged as unfit for further service.
Died at Kenilworth 21st February 1924.
Listed in the St Nicholas' Roll of Honour.

DYDE, William

Served in RAF in France 1915-1919. Died 1930.
Listed in the St Nicholas' Roll of Honour.

GARNER, J.

Name on the list of the Loyal Caledonian Corks Lodge of Oddfellows. No further information.

GRIFFITHS, Edward

Rifleman, 8430, 'C' Company, 4th Battalion, King's Royal Rifle Corps
Died 2nd March 1915, aged 24.
Buried in Voormezele Enclosure No. 3. Ypres, Belgium. II. C. 2.
Son of Mr George Edward and Mrs Charlotte Griffiths of Birmingham.
Brother of Mrs L. Webb of Whitemoor, Kenilworth. A native of Birmingham.
Listed in the St Nicholas' Roll of Honour.

HEWITT, James

Listed in the St Nicholas' Roll of Honour.

HUDSON, George John

Listed in the St Nicholas' Roll of Honour.

MARTIN, Ernest

Corporal, Royal Horse Guards (Blue).
Served in France with the Guards Divisional Police. Demobbed 4th March 1919.
Died at Kenilworth 28th July, 1924, aged 38.
A member of Warwickshire Police Force stationed at Kenilworth prior to the war.
Listed in the St Nicholas' Roll of Honour.

MILES, Alfred

Name given in the Parish Church Magazine, Roll of Honour, April 1918. No further information.

MOORE, J.

Name on the list of the Loyal Caledonian Corks Lodge of Oddfellows, and on the Working Men's Club Memorial. No further information.

REEVE, George Frederick

Died 1929. Listed in the St Nicholas' Roll of Honour.

STEWARD, George

Died 1930. Listed in the St Nicholas' Roll of Honour.

STRANGE, C.

Name on the Druid's Memorial. No further information.

Appendix III: Chronology of The Fallen

Those who died in 1914

13th September 1914, Edward Reeve
15th September 1914, William James Smith, age 23
19th October 1914, Henry Barnett, age 28
23rd October 1914, Sidney Charles Aitken, age 19
7th November 1914, Arthur Sawyer, age 23
12th November, 1914 James Thomas Stanley, age 22
19th December 1914, William Charles Hewitt, age 18
December 1914, Christopher Horsley, age 18

1915

21st February 1915 , Gilbert Percy Liggins, age 30
2nd March 1915, Edward Griffiths, age 24
10th March 1915, Frank Edward Feneran, age 33
6th April 1915, Sam Henry Insall, age 19
25th April 1915, William Wilkshire, age 33
25th April 1915, Frederick Bayliss, age 24
11th May 1915, Mervyn William Colomb
10th August 1915, John Cashmore, age 21
10th August, 1915, John W. Weyman, age 25
10th August 1915, Oswald Coke Winstanley, age 27
16th August 1915, Harry Cox, age 20
18th August 1915, Harold Christopher Bates, age 24
25th August 1915, Sidney Butler, age 22
25th September 1915, Albert Ernest Overton, age 26
25th September 1915, Frank Sabin, age 30
28th September 1915, Laurie Seekings, age 18
13th October 1915, Donald Ewen, age 28
3rd November 1915, Cuthbert George Llewellin Allen, age 32
12th December 1915, George Mitchner, age 19
30th December 1915, Francis Plant, age 52

1916

23rd April 1916, Albert Jaffray Cay, age 36
2nd May 1916, Harold Charles Martin, age 25
5th June 1916, Harry Mitchner, age 26
3rd July 1916, George Henry Swann, age 32
10th July 1916, Edward Whateley

13th July 1916, Herbert James Smith, age 23
14th July 1916, Charles Sydney Reed, age 29
18th July, 1916, Leonard Henry Reeve, age 24
25th July 1916, Alfred Reeve, age 32
1st August 1916, Thomas William Whateley
11th August 1916, Norman John Ward, age 21
18th August 1916, Henry Victor Gardner, age 20
18th August 1916, Thomas William Hickman, age 27
19th August 1916, William John Drane-Overs, age 29
28th August 1916, Walter John Barber, age 20
28th August 1916, Alfred Skelsey, age 43
29th August 1916, William Challoner, age 34
31st August 1916, Hubert Richard Faxon
3rd September 1916, Frederick Howlett Pittaway, age 27
15th September 1916, Trevor Carlyon Tweedy, age 21
18th September 1916, Edgar Thompson, age 22
26th September 1916, Guy Egerton Kidd DSO
30th September 1916, Charles Austin Butler, age 24
23rd October 1916, William Henry Watson
13th November 1916, Wilfred George Daniels, age 19
22nd November 1916, George Lushington Colomb DCM, age 27

1917

3rd January 1917, Jesse Mowe, age 20
8th January 1917, Charles Mowbray, age 27
18th January 1917, Leonard Henry Green, age 23
12th February 1917, Constance Mary Emily Seymour, age 29
2nd March 1917, William Charles Matthews, age 40
4th April 1917, Frederick Richard Wilkshire, age 20
14th April 1917, Walter Thomas Rawlins, age 36
24th April 1917, Arthur James Hubbard, age 27
26th April 1917, Alfred Aitken, age 26
28th April 1917, James Reynolds
8th May 1917, Harry Hincks, age 39
9th May 1917, Robert George Webster, age 20
10th May 1917, Edgar Arthur Vincent, age 20
10th June 1917, John Charles Morgan, age 34
13th June 1917, Charles Carter, age 21
12th July 1917, Reginald Carlyon Tweedy, age 48
13th August, 1917, Bertie Charles Bannard, age 27
22nd August 1917, Carlton Rivers, age 25

27th August 1917, Ernest Alfred Frazer, age 21
27th August 1917, William Jacob Parkyn, age 22
30th August 1917, Arthur Albert Sadler, age 26
5th September 1917, John Garrett, age 31
20th September 1917, E. Joseph Pratt, age 41
4th October 1917, James Pressley Tookey, age 36
4th October 1917, John Welch Bradshaw, age 32
9th October 1917, Ernest Letts, age 31
10th October 1917, Dudley Nevill White, age 20
12th October 1917, George Bricknell MM, age 37
2nd November 1917, William James West
10th November 1917, Reginald Dennis Clive, age 19
24th November 1917, Reginald Jack Collett, age 31
1st December 1917, Albert Edward Gillam, age 28
3rd December 1917, Harry Reynolds, age 38
22nd December 1917, Cyril William Carter, age 25

1918

6th January 1918, James Marvin, age 34
3rd February 1918, James Harris, age 34
12th February 1918, William Henry McCousins
2nd March, 1918, Ernest Thomas Ashmore, age 36
22nd March, 1918, Edward Vernon Barker
23rd March 1918, Charles Silvester Burton, age 36
23rd March 1918, Charles Harold Clifft, age 2
25th March 1918, William Beevers, age 20
25th March 1918, James Drew, age 22
3rd April 1918, Richard Henry Harris, age 36
11th April 1918, Charles William Newey, age 38
13th April 1918, William Henry Grainger, age 26
13th April 1918, Ernest H. Hopkins, age 26
25th May 1918, Arthur Henry Spicer, age 32
6th June 1918, Harry Lloyd Bidmead, age 23
8th June 1918, Walter Cannon
17th July 1918, Alfred George Nixon, age 38
19th July 1918, William Webb
31st July 1918, H. G. R. Boyt, age 19
22nd August 1918, John Stanley, age 19
23rd August 1918, Spencer Walton, age 19
29th August 1918, Harry Manton, age 22
13th September 1918, Edward John Webster, age 19

21st September 1918, George Henry Frazer, age 31
22nd September 1918, William Edward Eales, age 34
25th September 1918, Albert Edward Dilworth, age 19
25th September 1918, Albert Edward Buckingham, age 32
14th October 1918, Charles James Martin, age 22
14th October 1918, Sacheverel Darwin Wilmot, age 33
21st October 1918, Arthur Edgar Green, age 19
21st October 1918, Arthur Lake, age 30
24th October 1918, Charles Howard Gregory, age 22
25th October 1918, Frederick Daniel Mulcahy, age 36
28th October 1918, Harvey Warren, age 36
30th October 1918, Henry Oliver Edmond, age 28
22nd November 1918, William Alfred Jakeman, age 22

1919

26th February, William George Ward, age 19
23rd April, Victor Henry Drane, age 24
28th July, Arthur William Hazel, age 29
26th July, Harry Ellis, age 32
15th August, Frank Hewitt, age 21

1920

15th June, Austin Martin, age 34
13th August, Leonard Norman Parkyn

1923

5th September, Harry Stanley, age 43
31st December, Wilfred George Cox, age 30

1924

21st February, George Baterbee
28 July, Ernest Martin, age 38

1929

George Frederic Reeve

1930

William Dyde
George Steward

Appendix IV: Sources of Information

Primary Sources

Kenilworth St Nicholas' Church memorial book which until 2004 was on view in the church. It has now been removed for safe keeping and it is hoped that a copy will shortly be available.

Debt of Honour Register, The Royal Commonwealth War Graves Commission website, www.cwgc.org

Soldiers Died in the Great War 1914-1919 HMSO (available on CD rom)

Officers Died in the Great War 1914-1919 HMSO (available on CD rom)

The Kenilworth Advertiser newspaper 1910-1922 (on microfilm at Kenilworth library)

Coventry Herald newspaper 1914-1922 (on microfilm at Coventry library)

The Coventry Graphic 1914-1922 (on microfilm at Coventry library)

Warwick Advertiser newspaper 1914-1922 (on microfilm at Warwick library)

Kenilworth St Nicholas' church parish magazines 1914-1919

Kenilworth St John's church parish registers (held at Warwickshire County Record Office)

Kenilworth St Nicholas' church parish registers (held at Warwickshire County Record Office)

Spennell's Directories 1910, 1914 (held at Kenilworth Library)

Kelly's Directories 1912, 1916 (on microfilm at Kenilworth Library)

1891 Census (held at Kenilworth Library)

1901 census (on the internet at www.1901census.nationalarchives.gov.uk)

Secondary Sources

Martin Gilbert, *First World War*, 1995, Harper Collins.

Philip Warner, *World War One – a Chronological Narrative*, 1995, Brockhampton Press.

Lyn Macdonald, *1914 The Days of Hope*, 1989, Penguin Books.

Lyn Macdonald, *The Roses of No Man's Land*, 1993, Penguin Books.

Lyn Macdonald, *1915 The Death of Innocence*, 1997, PenguinBooks.

Lyn Macdonald, *Somme*, 1993, Penguin Books.

Lyn Macdonald, *They Called It Passchendaele*, 1993, Penguin Books.

Lyn Macdonald, *To the Last Man Spring 1918*, 1999, Penguin Books.

Martin Marix Evans, *Over The Top-Great Battles of The First World War*, 2002, Capella.

Robin Prior & Trevor Wilson, *Passchendaele – The Untold Story*, 2002, Yale University Press.

Chris McCarthy, *The Somme, the Day-by-Day Account*, 1993, Brockhampton Press.

John Laffin, *A Western Front Companion 1914-1918*, 1997, Sutton Publishing Ltd.

History of the 20th Century, World War I 1914-1918, 1993, Chancellor Press. (many different contributors).

Philip J. Haythornthwaite, *A Photohistory of World War One*, 1998, Brockhampton Press.

Simon Fowler, William Spencer & Stuart Tamblin, *Army Service Records of the First World War*, Public Record Office Readers' Guide No. 19, 1997, PRO Publications.

Norman Holding, *World War I Army Ancestry*, 3rd edition 1997, Federation of Family History Societies (Publishing) Ltd.

R. P. T. Davenport-Hines, *Dudley Docker, The Life & Times of a Trade Warrior*, 1984, Cambridge University Press.

Keith Beddoes, Colin & Stephen Wheeler, *Metro-Cammell 150 years of craftsmanship*, November 1999, Runpast Publishing.

John Drew, Kenilworth, *A Manor of the King*, 1994, Malcolm Peters.

Index